Diary of a Death Doula

25 Lessons the Dying Teach Us About the Afterlife

What people are saying about

Diary of a Death Doula

Death is never the end. Instead, it is a continuum of our journey, our consciousness—and always, our love. In this wise and hopeful book, Diamond shares her sacred work as a midwife to the dying, helping us understand the spiritual and emotional experience both of those transitioning, and those who support them. A clear, thoughtful book, sure to bring enormous comfort. **Sara Wiseman**, author of *Messages from the Divine: Wisdom for the Seeker's Soul*

Science rules the physical world, but the nonphysical belongs to the likes of Debra Diamond, a psychic Death Doula (with a PhD!) who goes where science rarely treads. Not full of "afterlife bunk" like so many such books are, Diamond's information comes from the demanding work she has chosen to do. *Diary of a Death Doula* is a straight-up and informative look at compassion, mediumship, the heavenly realm, and the acute possibility that our souls live after death. **Paul Perry**, author and coauthor of four *New York Times* bestsellers on near-death experiences

Having served as money manager, psychic medium, and death doula, Debra Diamond provides a unique perspective on dying and death, topics we tend to fear but that each of us needs to understand. This moving yet sensible book normalizes end-of-life experiences with real stories from real people to be a much-needed road map during our own or our loved ones' journeys. **Julie Beischel, PhD**, Director of Research, Windbridge Research Center

Through intimate storytelling, Dr. Diamond has gently released us from the debilitating heaviness of deep-seated cultural fears surrounding loss, death, dying, and perceived ontological uncertainties—veritably granting the permissions I think we all as humans wish for: the permission to be fully present in embracing this gift of life, and to walk our paths in levity guided by the innate knowing which connects us all. Dr. Diamond's *Diary of a Death Doula* is an exceptionally empowering and uplifting contribution to the body of work which will actively facilitate and hasten humanity's ongoing consciousness evolution.
Jill Hanson, founder and host, The Q.Psience Project

Debra Diamond writes with a comfortable style that allows the reader to enjoy the journey through the complex emotions and situations that surround the process of dying. With a gentle and compassionate tone, *Diary of a Death Doula* is not only a story of her experiences, but also a guide to help families and loved ones understand the processes involved in the death of the physical body. With the unique perspective of both a caregiver and a medium, the end of physical life is presented with an insight and detail that includes both the physical and spiritual connections between the patient, their families, caregivers and nonphysical beings who join in to facilitate the transition.
John G. Kruth, Executive Director, Rhine Research Center

Diary of a Death Doula

25 Lessons the Dying Teach Us About the Afterlife

Debra Diamond, Ph.D.

BOOKS

Winchester, UK
Washington, USA

JOHN HUNT PUBLISHING

First published by O-Books, 2019
O-Books is an imprint of John Hunt Publishing Ltd., 3 East St., Alresford,
Hampshire SO24 9EE, UK
office@jhpbooks.com
www.johnhuntpublishing.com
www.o-books.com

For distributor details and how to order please visit the 'Ordering' section on our website.

Text copyright: Debra Diamond 2018

ISBN: 978 1 78904 184 2
978 1 78904 185 9 (ebook)
Library of Congress Control Number: 2018967219

A CIP catalogue record for this book is available from the British Library.

Design: Stuart Davies

UK: Printed and bound by CPI Group (UK) Ltd, Croydon, CR0 4YY
US: Printed and bound by Thomson-Shore, 7300 West Joy Road, Dexter, MI 48130

We operate a distinctive and ethical publishing philosophy in
all areas of our business, from our global network of authors to
production and worldwide distribution.

Contents

About the author

Debra Diamond, Ph.D. is a psychic/medium and author. She's a former Wall Street money manager, CNBC commentator and Johns Hopkins University Professor who left a high profile life to pursue a life of spirituality and purpose. She earned an MBA from The George Washington University, a Masters Certificate from Christie's Education and a Ph.D. in Metaphysics from the Esoteric Interfaith Theological Seminary. She is the author of *Life After Near Death: Miraculous Stories of Healing and Transformation in the Extraordinary Lives of People With Newfound Powers.*

Dr. Diamond has been featured in the Wall Street Journal, Forbes, The Washington Post, The San Francisco Chronicle, Inc., The Baltimore Sun and NPR and other television, radio and broadcast programming.

Acknowledgements

Some say it takes a village to write a book. I am fortunate to have a team, both here and in the invisible realms, who helped me write *Diary of a Death Doula* to assist others in their time of need.

Daniel, Alex and Jed, thank you for your incredible help and support. I don't know what I did to deserve you but you make my world. You are special and I love you.

To Virginia McCullough, thank you for always knowing what I mean, even when I don't articulate it very well, and for your innate understanding of the material. You are a channel in your own way as well as being patient and kind.

Thank you, Phaedra Greenwood. I was actually looking for a painting group, not a writing group, but some divine providence led me to you instead. You are a remarkable person who always knows the answers and made a great impression on me.

To my classmates from that group, Jan Smith, Karen Baldwin, Abbie Conant and Brinn Colenda, your community provided the foundation for me to write my books.

For her wisdom on many levels, her support and suggestions, and all around wonderfulness, Sheila Kinkead, thank you. You helped me in many ways.

Susan Laubach, you are a person of so many talents, writing is just one of them. All those walks provided growth for me in the visible and invisible realms and I will always treasure our times together.

Kathy Kessler Overbeke. Thank you. I appreciate you in so many ways that I'd have to write another book to cover all the years.

Debbi Wilen Schwartz, you are a gem and one of the most caring people I know, besides being off the charts smart. Thank you for your steadfast support.

Thank you for everyone in the healing and helping professions for all you do. You are angels.

Author's Preface

Ten years ago, I had a transformative experience which led me to examine all my assumptions about the nature of reality, consciousness and life and death. Let me put it this way: To say my life was turned upside down would be a profound understatement. Everything I knew and did changed dramatically.

I left my high profile position as a money manager, CNBC commentator, and professor at Johns Hopkins University to pursue a life of purpose and spirituality. I became a psychic/medium and began to use my skills and gifts to help others and to explore the invisible realms beyond the material world.

As my journey progressed, my path continued to shift towards the direction of service to others, and one result has been my deep involvement in the world of hospice. In 2015, I became a hospice death doula, someone who sits bedside with the actively dying. Now, I've had the privilege and honor of spending time with many patients at end of life. There's no place I'd rather be — no work that is more rewarding.

Easing Fears of Death and Dying

The idea for *Diary of a Death Doula* came from what I experienced sitting bedside with the dying as a death doula, perceiving sacred realities. Because of our culture's fear of death, I thought it might be helpful if I could share stories about my work with you in the hopes it will alleviate your fears and anxieties about end of life and death, and provide comfort and information to all. (In the interest of privacy I've obscured or combined the identities and conditions of the patients.)

Being a death doula has given me a richer appreciation for life — and that's just one of the many lessons of this work.

I'll share more life lessons with you in the pages that follow and hope you find them as reassuring and inspiring as I do. Perhaps what I learned and experienced will change the way you think about life and death, open up the conversation and even challenge your own personal beliefs.

Ordinary and extraordinary

Working as a death doula is surprisingly life affirming, not morbid or sad as so many believe. Being in a hospice setting teeming with clinicians and specialists—nurses, aides, chaplains, and other volunteers—filling roles that might strike others as impossibly dreary, can be deceiving. Why would anyone willingly do this work? But like any other profession, there's more to it than meets the eye.

During the time I sit with the dying, extraordinary things can happen—or not much at all. The work is spiritual and sacred—but it's not for everyone. When I'm driving home at the end of my day, my concerns always seem to melt away as my perspective shifts and I give thanks for my many blessings.

In *Diary of a Death Doula*, I'll take you with me on what turned out to be a remarkable journey full of stories and insights and plenty of surprises. I'd like to think a different perspective about end of life and death will enable you to consider a new way of thinking of death, not as an end as so many believe, but as a continuation.

In *Diary of a Death Doula*, I look at death on three distinct planes: the physical, the soul, and the afterlife—but my perspective is unique. As a psychic/medium as well as a doula, I have the ability to bring the invisible realm into the visible and to recognize the interplay we don't often perceive through our five senses.

I bring an additional perspective as well, since I've spent many years researching and working with the phenomenon of the NDE—the near-death experience. Unlike my hospice work, working with the dying, the individuals who experience NDEs return to their bodies to continue life. I wrote about the near-death experience and consciousness in my first book, *Life After Near Death: Miraculous Stories of Healing and Transformation in the Extraordinary Lives of People With Newfound Powers*. That book examines life-altering NDE experiences through interviews with many individuals who've had them.

Now, in *Diary of a Death Doula*, I delve into not what we call "near-death," but actual death. Rather than being an unusual or strange experience to go from one situation to the other, I realized it was another leg of the same journey that allowed me to offer stories and insights about life, death, and the nature of consciousness.

In the end, I was given a much deeper look than I expected.

Introduction

Here's a question for you: *What would you think if we could take the fear and anxiety away from death and dying?* Do you think that's possible?

For many, the idea of decoupling fear and death seems nearly impossible. It's not the message most of us are used to hearing, even if we believe in the concept of some form of the afterlife. However, as a medium and death doula, I'm convinced more is going on in the realm of death and dying than most of us have been told or understand.

In my work at hospice, these patients didn't *tell* me about the process of dying, they *showed* me their journeys and those became the basis of the stories in this book. I share these extraordinary and profound stories with you in the hope they will open your mind to new possibilities too.

The questions

Sooner or later, everyone eventually asks questions about end of life:

What happens to me when my physical body dies? Is there an afterlife? If so, where do I go? Do my loved ones meet me? Will they usher me to the next plane of existence?

Young or old, single or married, rich, poor, or in between, we all seek answers to the essential questions of what lies ahead. Death itself is not only universal, even *thinking* about it is one of life's great equalizers.

What is death?

If you Google "death," what will you find? Wikipedia says, *"… a typically sad event because of the termination of social and familial bonds."* If you Google "dying," you might get the Oxford Dictionary definition, *"Ceasing to exist."*

I admit, neither of these sounds great, right? In our attempts to deny that death occurs, we've even gone so far as to adopt slang, like "passed" or "at peace" or "didn't make it," to avoid saying "death" or "dead" or "dying."

But what if these assumptions are wrong? What if death isn't a blank screen, a descent into nothingness? Or a one-way ticket to the "Horizontal Hilton"? What if we continue to exist, but the various "scenes" we've been told to picture are wrong? What if everything we "know" about death and dying isn't true? That our culture's limiting beliefs make end of life and death so scary?

What if...

The implications of a new way of looking at death are immense. Just imagine if the mainstream scientific community confirmed life after death. Think of the impact on science, religion, philosophy, and even the arts. On a personal level, consider how you might live if you knew *for sure* you were eternal. Think how it would free you to live unfettered by fear. Imagine what life might be like if we all incorporated the truths of eternal souls and related to each other through love, kindness, and consideration.

A new way to envision death and dying is available to everyone. It doesn't matter who you are or what culture you represent. From what I have seen and felt, people of all ages and backgrounds experience a vast realm of awe during this last stage of what we call life. In fact, a hidden journey takes place, and my work and abilities as a doula and medium make it possible to share this invisible reality with you. And it's nothing like what you've been told before.

Logically, you might think: *How does she know this?* This is probably just another stupid woo-woo or feel-good book. Or you're thinking this book can't possibly help me. *I've lost loved ones and I've watched family members suffer and die. I don't buy this. Not for a minute.*

Fair enough, but I hope you'll keep reading, Perhaps you'll

think, *Maybe, just maybe, there's something to this.*

The ways of modern death

As science has come to occupy a prominent place in Western culture, our relationship with death has been altered. In our scientific culture, death has been translated into a soulless, clinical experience that strikes fear into the heart of almost everyone.

Some of us readily admit we're afraid of the pain of actually dying, while others aren't afraid of death, but become anxious thinking about the unfathomable—it's like a picture we can't quite bring into focus. Some of the most rational and intelligent individuals I know simply refuse to talk about death in the belief that those discussions will bring it on sooner. So not only does the physical process bring us discomfort, but the role of superstition and "tempting fate" is also a factor. No wonder most conversations about death are almost too much for most of us to handle.

Who answers the questions?

These days many of us believe that science can explain almost anything. We count on science to explain how we approach our day-to-day existence, communicate with each other, maintain our physical bodies, make decisions, fall in love, and tell us about our place as humans in the universe.

In fact, in our Western culture, science has become so powerful it has extended its hold to our views of death and end of life. How we think about death has become heavily influenced by the fact that death is largely treated in medical settings where we're viewed as diseases and treatments rather than patients. Going even further, patients can also be viewed as evidence of "failure," the failure of science to stop death in its tracks. We repeat phrases like, "Where there's life there's hope," even when we know that isn't strictly true. We may declare ourselves fighters who will beat a disease, because that disease often leads to death. Given all that, is it any wonder we often view death as an antiseptic event we not only will do almost anything to avoid, but approach as if it's the enemy?

Yes, scientific pursuits have given us the chance to improve the human condition. No doubt about it. However, since science is primarily helpful in our dealings with the observable universe, it has its limitations. Because what transpires in death and dying is largely outside the observable universe. The invisible exists within the visible, and this cannot be understood by pure observation.

There's more at play at end of life and death than meets the eye. We can't weigh and measure it or classify it into scientific categories, and we can't examine it under a microscope or in a CT scan. That's why we need to remove the limitations of the physical body and create another vision of death and perhaps even another language to describe it.

How do we deal with death?

Since death isn't like other issues, we can't problem solve our way out of it. So we attempt to deal with it by avoiding it altogether, and fool ourselves (at least temporarily) that these tactics will make it go away and not happen to us! We're kept apart—or choose to be apart—from death. Let's face it: death is an ill-fitting suit we'd rather not try on.

Because we lack a full frontal acceptance of death, talking about it is mostly taboo. It's hardly the go-to topic around the Thanksgiving dinner table, even if someone in the family is gravely ill. In fact, that might make everyone go to even greater lengths to avoid mentioning it. And with great success I might add.

But does it have to be this way? I don't believe so, and all the research I've done and experiences I've had tell me we *can* dial back the fear. I wrote this book to show you how. And to advance the conversation about a new twenty-first century view of death.

Wait! Do you mean we can change our perspective on death?

Absolutely. The reset I'm talking about starts with information that changes our thinking and allows us to consider death 2.0 rather than death 0.0. So I start with the premise that it's time for a different way of looking at, thinking about, and dealing with death. A new understanding of death is nothing less than an opportunity to transform ourselves both personally and collectively. And the process starts with redefining death.

A medium's perspective on death and what's "beyond"

As I said earlier, I'm a psychic and a medium, and that means I deal with the unseen world in order to offer proof of survival beyond death. Mediums are a link between dimensions — that's the nature of our gift.

As you can imagine, a medium's perspective is very different from the scientific or the Western medical model. We mediums believe in the spiritual, the possibilities that exist beyond our knowing and the evidence and information we are able to capture outside the bounds of ordinary reality.

As a medium, I have the ability to access information beyond the usual sensory inputs and give a concrete essence to places that are by nature hard to picture. As a clairvoyant, I bring a special perspective to the study of death and dying since I'm frequently able to see "happenings" not observable by the naked eye. For me, receiving this information is like how most people see or breathe. It's like having another sense. At first, it scared and confused me, but now I don't even question it.

Mediums work in the nonphysical realm, just as the scientific community works in the realm of measurable observations. So, to approach this work of death and dying as a medium, we must first understand that dying is not an ordinary state of consciousness, not measurable, weighable, or quantitative. It's an altered state requiring us to think in terms of dimensions beyond our three-dimensional world. This is a difficult concept for many to grasp, but particularly tough for the scientific community. The lack of acceptance of this altered state concept is also one of the primary reasons why the study of death and dying hasn't advanced significantly in the twentieth century or in this early part of the twenty-first. The notion that we can exist in multiple dimensions is too great of a leap for many, and especially true for many mainstream scientists.

Based on my ability as a medium and doula, I can acknowledge the role of energy in the universe and understand the reality that life on earth is but one small part of the overall picture. As I see it, rather than excluding science, my viewpoint complements it.

As a medium and death doula, I am able to see the concerns of the dying and what is important to them. I'm also able to see who is with them, and their soul's journey. As a result of what I've had the privilege of seeing, feeling, and knowing, I'm less afraid of death and more open to the possibilities that lie beyond.

Some people think what I do is hocus-pocus. Others think it's cray-cray. That's okay. My job is not to convince you. But if you believe in this other realm, are inclined to, or have had some experience yourself, you will know what I'm telling you is true. Even if you don't believe in any form of life beyond death and think the notion of the afterlife is bunk, that's okay too. Hopefully you'll still take something away by your willingness to keep an open mind.

About this book

What you'll find in these pages is a description of the full range of my duties as a death doula, from my training and interactions with patients and families, to the life lessons I learned from the dying. In *Diary of a Death Doula*, you'll read how our loved ones in Spirit are waiting in the wings to meet and attend to the dying.

You'll learn you don't have to be very spiritual or religious to experience the love, and how the meaning of life is revealed to the dying. I also describe the way the spirit leaves the body at end of life to go on its journey.

In addition, I talk about the 24/7 world of hospice, from the interdisciplinary care to the teams who treat the patients. And, of course, I'll discuss the metaphysical and spiritual encounters that confirm we are more than our physical bodies. The continuation of life, the survival of the soul and the role the Universe plays run through all these stories. What I've learned from all my work and that I'll share with you is that *your soul continues on with or without your physical body*.

Here's even better news: *Your soul grows and interacts on a much higher and richer plane once we pass.*

So whether it's off to heaven for eternity or to come back around, whether you pass peacefully at 100 or suddenly at a younger age, my work affirms what many have been taught and provides good news to the skeptics: *Yes, we continue; our essence endures.*

This book is divided into four parts:

In Part One, I examine cultural beliefs about death and the impact of science and religion on our views of death.

In Part Two, I tell you a little about my background and explain the basic definitions of hospice and death doulas.

In Part Three, I present cases—stories—of patients at end of life, their journeys and the lessons we all can learn from the dying. Following each case are passages, "Sacred Reflections," summarizing key points to keep in mind about what I observed and noted from my experiences, including healing and spiritual ideas. Perhaps you will open up to these ideas and think about them after you close the book.

In Part Four, I examine consciousness at end of life and in the afterlife. I step back and explain how serving as a death doula has affected me and how we can consider a new, updated twenty-first century view of death.

The first part of the book aims to lay a foundation for this work and an understanding of what hospice does. However, if you're mainly interested in the patient stories, you might skip ahead to Part Three and bypass the technical explanations of hospice and my background as a medium. You can always come back and read it later.

At the end of the day, this is the journey of all of us; the story of our relationship with the universe, reality, and consciousness. It's not easy to comprehend what we call death and the mysteries of the universe, but I hope this diary helps you understand our essential energetic nature and that our souls seem connected to a much larger reality.

Is death an existentialist mystery? Or is the answer right here, just beyond us?

Part One

A Cultural History of Death—It Wasn't Always Taboo

In the ancient world, human cultures were open to the mysteries of life; in some cases, more open than we are today. Our ancestors had respect for the invisible world, if for no other reason than their lack of an alternative explanation for virtually all natural phenomena. It was routine for ancient cultures to revere and respect the dead and they were commonly included in the lives of the living and even consulted for guidance. Sometimes they were treated in death as if they were still alive.

In ancient cultures the idea that the soul survived death was well accepted. Descriptions of communities of spirits, underworlds, heaven and realms of the dead were incorporated into life. Many of these beliefs continued throughout history and cultures for thousands of years. Not until we reach more modern times do these beliefs begin to be questioned or disregarded.

The Incas preserved their dead, sought their guidance, and even put them in chairs and carried them to parties and other social events. The Mayans buried their dead below the living room floor, to keep them involved as an extension of the family. This veneration of the ancestors stemmed partly from the belief that the dead continued to exist and partly as a way to ensure the ancestors' continued well-being.

Like the Mayans and the Incas, the Mesopotamians, going back in 3100 BCE, believed the dead continued an animated existence in the form of spirit. According to the Mesopotamians, the soul reunites with relatives who precede them in death, which is consistent with what I witnessed as a death doula. Anthropologists have discerned that nearly 2,500 years ago, the Mesopotamians believed that the soul was not immediately transported to the netherworld after bodily death, but had to undergo an arduous journey in order to reach it.

The ancient Egyptians believed that even in death they would live again, and these ideas are in many ways similar to what I encountered as a death doula. The continuity of life was demonstrated over and over in my work as patients traveled to their new home, visiting with family and loved ones on the other side, taking their beliefs, memories, and essence with them. To the Egyptians, death was the necessary first step to reaching the afterlife, a journey they prepared for thoroughly during their lifetimes.

Even in more recent Victorian times, death was openly discussed and mortality was confronted head-on. Death in those times was described as a journey of passage where the near and dear were ultimately heaven bound. Elaborate displays were part of the Victorian celebration of death and the advent of photography even enabled mourners to pose with the dead laid out in their coffins before they set off for burial.

Up until the twentieth century, most people died at home with family and friends around them. Death was an accepted part of life. Nowadays, we live much longer and prefer to lean towards the working hypothesis that medicine and healthy living—exercise, stress reduction and good nutrition—will prolong our lives and, psychologically speaking, that death won't actually happen to us!

The Impact of Religion On Our Beliefs About Death

It's really hard to talk about death and dying without some mention of religion and its power to comfort some, but strike fear in others. What about your own attitudes and apprehensions about death and dying? You may be religious and approach the subject with certain beliefs, or perhaps you count yourself among the growing number with no particular religious affiliation but are not an atheist either?

Undoubtedly, different religions and cultures and our own

individual "buy in" of these beliefs greatly influence our views of life and death. Regardless of what they are, these values are drummed into most people from a very early age, and many find that later in life, they may begin to question these "truths." As a result, as we age, how we think of life and death can change dramatically.

Today in the West, we have no uniform religious or cultural beliefs, so we have no specific place where we believe everyone goes after death. We don't even have a uniform language for dying. Some simply say their loved ones died; others say they passed or passed over or made their transition or have gone home. The complex attitudes and language in the West arise from this "hodgepodge" of different cultures, theories, and religions all coming together to form our diverse society. Our wide-ranging beliefs include everything from reincarnation to purgatory to nirvana, and many gradations of each. We wrestle with and accommodate an unnerving combination of ideas and definitions.

Each religion has developed their own narrative over thousands of years to explain something that seems inexplicable. As you can see, relying on religion doesn't provide a simple answer about what happens to us.

The Scientific View of Death

In contrast with religion, mainstream science has developed its own views of death, and as expected, they don't intersect much with more spiritual views. While some religions speak of a soul and spiritual consciousness, science generally doesn't endorse the concept that consciousness survives death. Actually, science can't even define consciousness—and they offer no definition for what we'd typically call "an extraordinary experience." Science requires proof, and these experiences and the notion of eternal life don't easily lend themselves to the proof designed to satisfy the scientific model.

The scientific method requires consistent corroboration and reproduction, but if you've ever had an extraordinary experience or even a dream, you know they can't be reproduced at will. Dreams and visions and even gut hunches are spontaneous events, and that's essentially the nature of our connection with the universe.

Likewise, consciousness itself is not standardized, and you'll see abundant evidence of that throughout this book. In short, consciousness can't be reproduced; it's dynamic, fueled by energy and as unique as each one of us. And that's precisely why the concept is problematic for science.

So, even to begin the discussion of what death actually is, we have to accept that death is a state we can't define. And beyond looking at physical, measurable signs, science can't explain it, either. Death, and consciousness itself, is as much a philosophic issue as a scientific one, and perhaps one day, we can resolve the whole matter in a realm not yet developed.

Part Two

A Spiritual Journey

My story with hospice began seventeen years ago when my mother was close to death, and we called hospice in during those final weeks and days. Hospice made a profound impression on all of us, but especially me.

Before my mother passed, I'd never been close to death. Up to that point I'd never seen anyone die. I didn't understand that dying can go on for days, weeks, months. Nor did I realize that no profound last words are uttered, and the heavens don't open spectacularly, either.

When I was growing up, we weren't allowed to attend funerals—it was considered bad luck. On the day of the funeral, we'd be shuttled off to a family member or friend's house. But I always wondered, *What was the mystery all about? What was I missing?*

Prior to my mother's passing, my idea of death was based on what I'd seen in the movies. A lightning bolt would announce death. It would be something dramatic and startling. The heavens would open up and all the secrets of the Universe would be revealed. Naturally, I soon found out this view of death was an illusion, appropriate for the big screen, but not at all like actual death.

The dying process isn't like what we see in the movies or on TV. It's a process, just like birth. It takes a great deal of energy to die since we aren't simply moving ahead with life. That would take energy enough. Instead, we're moving ahead to another realm and that requires us to reorder our body and our essence to get there. In some sense, the easiest step is leaving our body. The line between life and death is blurred, because there really is no line. We shift, we move on, but we still exist.

Our consciousness at the end of life

As I watched my mother during her last days, I noticed she spent most of her time elsewhere. She wasn't talking about her needs or sharing her thoughts, and she seemed to be in another "place." I wasn't sure where she was or who she was talking to, but I knew she was experiencing something unlike any aspect of death I'd ever heard of. She seemed to be traveling to a place where she was clearly participating and engaged. Looking back, I realize now there are senses beyond hearing that exist at end of life.

When we witness our loved ones sleeping at end of life, this is when they are actually hard at work, preparing for the new realm they will transition to. This is an important part of moving on. It's invisible to most people, but trust me, I've seen dying men and women do this preparatory work and it's a real process that allows them to adapt when they finally cross over.

In this preparation stage, we're given a glimpse of our new home, to help us become familiar and comfortable with what's ahead. While visiting this new place, we'll see recognizable, meaningful sights, which could include our families and loved ones, or others from our lives. Whoever and whatever we see, we'll have personally meaningful experiences that help create the bridge necessary to transition.

Hospice makes an impression

Hospice made an impression on me—an impression beyond the one that death makes on all of us. *Perhaps this was meant to be*, I've mused over the years, and especially as I began my work with hospice.

One day, when the hospice nurse came to visit my mother, she handed me a piece of paper. "You should read this," she said.

I assumed the note was about medications or equipment, or perhaps advice about funeral arrangements. Eventually, I looked at the paper the nurse handed me. It said:

If the body is ready and the soul isn't, you don't leave.
If the soul is ready and the body isn't, you don't leave.
When the soul is ready and the body is ready, then you leave.

I thought about this. It was a new way to look at death. Rather than a single event, this hospice professional was telling me that death is a process involving two separate contracts, body and soul.

I read the paper again, and thought more about it. In fact, I thought about it for the next 15 years. I knew then that one day I wanted to work with hospice. I didn't know in exactly what capacity, but I knew that I wanted to be of service. I also knew this was something that I was capable of doing and that I'd be comfortable working with the dying.

A transformational experience

People often ask, "Have you always been a psychic and medium?" Actually, I can say I always *knew* things. I just didn't know a descriptive label could be applied. When I was younger, I didn't understand my abilities and figured I just had "good instincts." I never aspired to be a medium. I didn't grow up thinking, "Gee, I hope I get to be a psychic or medium one day!" I pursued another path as a money manager, a Professor of Investments at Johns Hopkins University, and a CNBC commentator.

When I was in the money management business, my boss used to say, "Debra, you have great instincts." I decided that must be the answer. Yes, great instincts! Years later I found out my ability involved so much more. As I came to understand it, my gifts were beyond the ordinary.

Before I delve into my work as a death doula and medium, let me tell you about the transformational event I experienced. It's significant because it was the catalyst that led to a shift that meant leaving my successful career in the financial arena to pursue work as a psychic/medium and eventually a death doula. It set the wheels in motion for everything that followed.

In 2008, I had an experience that left me with unconventional powers as a clairvoyant. To be clear about this, I didn't go looking for an extraordinary experience. In fact, I didn't even know what an extraordinary experience was. Briefly, here's what happened. I took an intuition development class in New York, because I figured I had pretty good intuition and it would be fun to give it a tune-up.

At one point in the class, after we did several elementary exercises, our teacher announced that we were going to do a séance. I consulted the schedule. *A séance? No way!* I thought I was here to learn telepathy. And maybe a few tools to enhance my intuition. I reconsidered and resigned myself to doing this one séance and moving on to the next exercise. *What did I have to lose? Nothing was going to happen anyway.*

The teacher guided the class into a meditative state and said she'd take us out of the meditation in a few minutes. She also said if we "saw" anything, we should let her know and she would tell us what to do next. I *knew* I wouldn't see anything, and as I meditated with the class, I felt the wooden chair pressing up against my back, the warm air circulating in the room, and the taxis honking on 7th Avenue. A few minutes later, the teacher brought us out of our meditation.

"Okay. Does anyone 'see' anything?" she asked.

I looked around the room. Everyone was looking at each other. I raised my hand.

"Yes, Debra. What do you see?" the teacher asked.

"I see about 50 people," I said. I explained I saw my relatives who had passed. I saw friends and relatives of classmates in the room. I also saw random people, including 42nd Street showgirls and pushcart peddlers strolling across the room. There was a whole vibrant world unfolding in front of me, invisible but as real as this one.

The teacher then asked, "Do you see anyone in the corner of the room? Because if you see someone in the corner, they probably go with someone sitting in that corner."

"I do," I said. "I see someone in the right corner."

She asked me to describe the person and I described a Hispanic man in his 20s, with long dark hair parted in the middle and a big, handlebar mustache. As I described him, the woman in the corner began to sob.

"I can identify him," she said. "He was my fiancé." She wanted to know if I could identify him from pictures she had on her cell phone.

I said I could, so during the break she flipped through her pictures. "There!" I said, pointing at a picture of a dark-haired man with a handlebar mustache. "That's him!"

"Yes," she replied. "That's him. I've wanted to connect with him since he passed but I never heard from him. I was so disappointed." As she hugged me, she thanked me for making the connection she so desperately wanted. She was thrilled about what happened in the session.

An unwanted shift

Now remember, I come from Wall Street. There are no hugs on Wall Street. And no thank you's either. I wasn't accustomed to the kind of reaction I got from this young woman. But it wasn't lost on me that I'd done something meaningful for her and had made a connection she'd longed for. I was shaken up but I was also grateful—not to mention stunned and overwhelmed.

It took me months to deal with this experience. I didn't discuss it with anyone, choosing to try to ignore it. I didn't have an explanation or context for what happened and no idea of what to make of it. As time went on, though, I began to understand that I was working with energy. That we are energy and that everything is energy. My gift is my ability to connect to our energetic essence.

Over time, I not only adjusted to my new talents and abilities, I learned to embrace these gifts, to speak to those who had passed and work with the energy I was given. In time, as I became comfortable with my abilities, I relaxed about the connections I was able to make. I began to do readings, lecture, write, and establish a practice as a psychic/medium. In fact, I've even come to think of myself as normal, which shows just how far I've come.

My profound personal transformation, which began in an intuition class in New York, became the foundation of my work.

My transition to work with the other side

In my journey from money manager to medium and hospice death doula, Spirit—the unseen energies of the universe— and consciousness have always been the chief protagonists driving my abilities. Yet, even as I adjusted to life after my transformational experience in 2008, these unseen forces didn't let up. They had other plans for me, and in 2013, they began to reveal them, leading to my work with near-death experiencers and my book, *Life After Near Death: Miraculous Stories of Healing and Transformation in the Extraordinary Lives of People With Newfound Powers*. My deep involvement in the world of NDEs continues to this day.

Yet, even as I continued my work as a medium and author, hospice was still stuck in my mind. I wanted to be of service, specifically through hospice. I began looking into hospice training programs, and finally enrolled in one in 2015. I was comfortable with death and was sure I could work with the dying as a death doula. After all, as a medium I could already communicate with the other side.

As I began my work as a doula, sitting bedside with the dying, my path opened once again. What started as an opportunity to be of service spring-boarded into a totally immersive experience using my powers to experience what occurs at end of life. And that subsequently became the driving force for this book.

A journey to other dimensions

What I'm about to tell you is quite unusual, even for someone who deals in the paranormal. As a medium, I communicate with those who have passed. You might be familiar with other mediums who do that, too. Some have written books or appeared on television. But my experience differs because as a death doula, who is also a medium, I see our souls *journeying* at end of life and also see family members and loved ones *in Spirit* who come in to help patients transition. I can't emphasize this enough. I'm not surprised by any of this, since as a medium, I speak to those who have passed and they relate their journeys and experiences while dying and reveal the work they are engaged in on the other side.

The idea that consciousness survives physical death is not new, and many have explored it. However, the stories in this book ask you to reconsider these assumptions in light of the evidence I've gathered. As I sat with patients, I began to understand the experiences they had at end of life, regardless of age, gender, religion, or belief.

Through my work, I learned that as we move on, our ego dissolves and our consciousness emerges and carries on in an expansive environment not dependent on the physical body. I have seen this. *I have seen it with all of the patients I sat with as a death doula.* Some silently communicate with me and tell me about their journeys. Meanwhile, as I keep vigil, their families in spirit also communicate with me.

Many people have a belief that something else exists and there is something more "out there," and my experience as a doula further confirmed this to me. There is a piece of us that is infinite, and I witnessed that as I sat with the dying. That part of us is eternal, and represents a vast intelligence. That world isn't far, far away. We are always close to it. It is right here, next to us, and we only need to shift to feel it.

The Role of Hospice

Most people have had an experience with hospice or are at least familiar with the concept. They may have had a family member or friend in hospice and know that hospice care is designed to reduce pain and manage symptoms for people who are terminally ill at end of life.

While different types of hospice are available, such as long-term care, home hospice, and hospitalized settings, this book's focus is on in-patient hospice. My experiences took place in a facility in which those with a terminal illness spend their last days, and patients who are given six months or less to live receive palliative care.

Most private insurers cover the costs of hospice, but it's also paid for through the Medicare or a Medicaid Hospice Benefit program. In 2014, approximately 2.6 million people died in the United States, and approximately 1.6 million patients received hospice care from one of the more than 5,500 hospice programs in the US.

Many individuals are afraid the first time they walk through the door of a hospice. They expect something funereal or depressing but hospice is generally a relaxed setting that may not even seem like a health care facility. Instead, these facilities are full of life and compassion, and are designed to be as comfortable and "homey" as possible.

My work as a doula takes place in a warm, inviting atmosphere where tasteful artwork graces the hallways, and baskets of freshly baked cookies are scattered throughout the facility. All the patients' rooms have access to beautiful gardens, along with plenty of quiet spaces for quiet contemplation. Unlike typical hospitals, relatives can visit at any time, and even stay overnight. The space is relaxed and low key, with a quiet energy about it, a significant accomplishment considering the backdrop is something most people find terrifying.

In the last few years, hospice programs have increasingly recognized the mind-body-spirit connection, which in turn has led to offering practices such as Healing Touch, Reiki, or Mindfulness. Still, within hospice, we're just at the tip of the iceberg with these new spiritual practices. If you have a family member or loved one in any hospice program, make sure you ask if these services are available.

You don't have to spend much time at hospice to realize how dedicated the nurses are. After I volunteered several times, many of them thanked me. Why are they thanking me? I wondered. After all, I didn't really do anything. But, as they explained, they grow close to the patients but aren't able to be with them all the time, especially at the end. So a volunteer who can sit with an actively dying patient provides the nursing staff and the family the peace of mind that their loved one is not alone. As for me, I know dying is a part of life, a time of great reverence, a spiritual and quiet period. It's nothing less than an honor to be a part of hospice.

What Exactly Is a Death Doula?

While not providing medical care, death doulas support patients at end of life and offer comfort to the dying. By definition, doulas are accepting and comfortable being with someone whose life is ending. That is the essence of our work, but words can't really sum up the experience. That's the reason I wrote a book largely comprised of patient stories that I hope leave you with a better understanding of our work, the work of hospice and the unfolding journey at end of life.

As a doula, I need to be a calming and peaceful presence, which can help make the experience not quite as scary and difficult for patients and family members and loved ones. Integral to our work is reassuring the dying and those around them that everything is going the way it should.

Earlier I described my work as a death doula as sacred and surprisingly life affirming. The time sitting bedside is usually quiet and still, although things can change rapidly. It's also a process in which extraordinary things can happen—or nothing much at all.

Some death doula programs are called "11th hour" or "vigil programs," but my program is a "Death Doula" program, so named because it's similar in concept to the work of birth doulas. Birth doulas stay with women through labor and delivery, and usher a newborn into life; death doulas sit with patients at end of life and usher them out. Those who have been present for a birth and a death often express their surprise when they experience the same sense of sacredness in the room at both events.

No one knows the exact number of death doulas serving today, but it's likely around several thousand. Although the concept is relatively new, training programs have sprung up in the last few years as demand for doula services has increased. It isn't surprising that the numbers are still small, because few people know about death doulas, and even the hospice concept is relatively new to many.

Put simply, a death doula has something the palliative care nurse does not have. Time. Time to sit with the patient without distractions. Since nurses are busy with other patients and duties—and families are often dealing with many issues— doulas are focused on supporting the patient when others may not be able to do so.

The day-to-day work of death doulas

The first time I walked into the room of an actively dying patient, I was shocked. It was awful. A barely-breathing patient was prone on the bed, eyes half-closed or rolled back. I was sure he was in pain. However, I have since learned this is simply how the body shuts down, one part at a time. It's a natural part of the process.

As I sit bedside with a patient, I may hold his hand lightly or swab her mouth. Mostly I sit quietly as patients lie in bed observing other realms, filled with visions that are meaningful and familiar to them. Their loved ones in Spirit play a role in this process as well, in what the medical establishment calls "visions" or "visitations." Many patients are aware their loved ones in Spirit are with them and are comforted by this.

There are some patients who are clear about wanting to die alone without their families or friends present, while others who come directly from nursing homes or assisted living to hospice may have no one left to be with them. In that situation, death doulas are there to make sure no one needs to die alone. This is one of the most valuable services doulas provide.

In some programs, doulas assist with funeral arrangements; or help patients get their wills and advance directives together. However, my program does not include these services. My job is to be the eyes and ears of the staff and family, an end-of-life or transition guide, to provide comfort and support.

How I experience death doula work

As a doula, I generally don't know who I will meet when I step into a patient's room. There's always a bit of anxiety about what I'll find on the other side of the door. However, I center myself and try to maintain a clear energy before knocking lightly, and once inside the room, I introduce myself to the patient and generally pull up a chair. I speak softly, assuring patients that I'm there to be with them. Patients generally don't respond, but I'm sure they are aware of me.

Of course, I also do some ordinary things too, like making sure patients are comfortable and warm under the soft blankets. I speak to them in a normal tone of voice. If I believe they won't be disturbed, I might hold their hand or stroke their arm. Generally though, I sit quietly, because this special work requires being still for long periods of time.

While the doula is generally there to support the patient during the end-of-life process, they may also provide support for loved ones. End of life can be a complex and emotionally demanding time, and the last moments of life can be filled with difficult issues and mystifying feelings. Many families are nervous and anxious. They may be under great stress as a result of all they've been through that led to their loved one entering hospice in the first place. I might offer to get them a cup of coffee or just sit and chat. Many families just want someone to listen while they unburden themselves. This is a satisfying part of the work, because it's another way of helping people when they most need support. I discovered that many family members and friends of patients had never seen anyone die before, so having someone to whom they can voice fears and ask questions makes a huge difference.

Sometimes I'll ask family and friends about their loved one. "Tell me about your mother," I might say. Or, "What is your friend like?" Sometimes this kind of conversation is welcomed, but I don't take it personally if friends and family decline to answer.

Although this work doesn't make me uncomfortable, I understand when others say they'd be uneasy in this role. For all kinds of reasons, death makes almost everyone uncomfortable.

How others react when they hear I'm a death doula

People react in various ways when I tell them what I do. Usually a certain look comes over their faces and their eyebrows shoot up. Most everyone says, "Wow!" or seems surprised. A few seem alarmed, but others are fascinated by death—in an abstract kind of way. Some people want to know everything, eager for the gory details. Sometimes they ask, "Have you ever seen anyone die?" (Unsurprisingly, the answer is yes.) Almost no one truly understands what I do, because fear and anxiety inform their understanding of death, even if they want to believe death is natural and sacred.

When I'm at a party, for example, and I mention I'm a death doula, I'm usually struck by how abnormal this work seems to others. Some walk away. Others clasp their hands over their heart and say, "You must be a very special person."

Then they walk away!

The realities of death

Being a death doula is not what people think. For example, before I started this work, I assumed the patients in hospice would be a lot older than me. However, that assumption quickly evaporated when I began to encounter many people younger—a lot younger—than I am. This still gives me pause, leading me to reflect on my own mortality. I often look at the patient roster and birthdates, and note the presence of those younger individuals. And here they are at the end of life.

Of course, on an intellectual level we all know that young people and children die, but we still picture death as coming to those who live to a ripe old age. I can tell you firsthand, seeing the younger patients at hospice brings home the truth that death is not only the great equalizer, it's also a reality check.

Many people believe an aura of mystery is present at the time of death, whether or not they can clearly perceive it. And yes, there's an energy unlike any other present in the rooms of the dying and it's felt as soon as we walk through the door. It's the air of the sacred. No one can do this work without a sense of being in touch with something potent that transcends much of what we know and understand about the human condition. There is a power in these moments that eclipses ordinary earth time. I've felt it in every room.

This mystery and "unlike-any-other" energy is probably the reason most are unsure about what to expect when they first begin working as a doula. Apprehension is common among new doulas. When I began this work I wondered, will the patients want to go over their regrets, unburden themselves, have deep penetrating conversations, or even open up about now being enlightened? Will patients possess some newfound wisdom, the kind we all seek? Will the volunteer encounter a transcendent experience?

Well, to be honest, not really. Generally, none of those topics ever comes up.

Instead, while they're in service, some doulas meditate; others watch TV or listen to music. Some read poetry or the Bible. I usually read or meditate or sit quietly. Since patients are often in a deep sleep and probably medicated, many don't talk at all and may not even move very much. But that doesn't matter. Death doulas are still at work doing their service.

What kind of person becomes a death doula?

Doulas are women and men who come from all backgrounds and walks of life. Many are brought to service after a loved one has passed and they want to give back as a way of showing gratitude. Others go into this work out of the desire to do something meaningful with their lives. As you'd expect, many doulas are retired, usually in their fifties, sixties or older, and available to come to hospice or a patient's home and sit for hours or even overnight. I've not seen many young faces in the doula crowd.

Doula shifts can last two to eight hours, but any amount of time is appreciated. The midnight shift especially loves volunteers, since family and friends may leave the facility in the evening, and quite often, no one is available to be with the patient through the night. Many of us don't leave a patient or walk out at the end of a shift unless we know someone else is coming in after us.

As for religious affiliation, doulas come from all religious backgrounds or they might be agnostic. Many would describe themselves as spiritual, and it's possible they've had a transformational experience themselves that changed the way they want to use their lives. I know that was true for me.

What it takes to be a doula

Being a doula requires patience—lots of it. For the most part, the doula is sitting quietly, being with the spiritual nature of what is unfolding. Doulas also need to be patient because death takes its time. Since doulas serve all types of people, it's important they be accepting and nonjudgmental. Doula work can stir up personal experiences, so being emotionally comfortable helps a doula handle the sometimes surprising or disturbing responses. While I sat with many patients who died, I found that each death takes a certain processing and each one transformed me a little more.

As valuable as training programs are, no one can teach a person to be a doula. The training provides information and valuable guidance, but over the long-term, a doula's success depends on what he or she brings to the table. As I've said, this work is not for everyone. I've certainly had to search within myself to examine how to respond to those who fear death, and how to deal with the physical aspects of a dying patient, which can be frightening if you're not accustomed to them.

Sitting bedside can have a powerful, moving kind of beauty to it, which is not sad or morbid. Some doulas say that as a result of their experiences, they've come to live more fully. Sitting with the dying creates meaning from loss, and it raised my awareness and appreciation for life. For me and for many doulas, the overall experience is one of love and peace and giving back.

The work is rich, sometimes mundane, but always gratifying. It's critical to remember the experience of end of life is part of life. For the most part, the doula's work is sitting with someone who is still alive.

What's a Medium?

I am a doula but I am also a medium. Of course, not all doulas are mediums, but because I am, I can relate my work across both disciplines. I can fill you in about what we mediums do and how our work is special.

A medium is someone who communicates with those who've passed. Mediums may hear, see, sense, or feel those on the other side, and we convey information from those in the Spirit world through our higher connections and sensitivities.

The folks I meet on the other side are people, just like you and me. They're interested in sharing their wisdom and experience, and connecting with loved ones on earth. Those on the other side can be a chatty bunch and if there's something they want us to know, they can be insistent about getting their message through. Or course, they need someone to help them do this and that's where mediums come in.

A medium/death doula's perspective

When I contact those who have already passed as a medium, they are usually settled in and able to converse and reflect on what they've learned on the other side. They often have messages for their loved ones on Earth, and they want us to know that they love us, that they're okay and that they're still here.

As a death doula who is also a medium, I'm able to "see" what transpires in the invisible world at end of life. I also communicate with those loved ones in Spirit who arrive to provide support and comfort and accompany the dying as they move on. My abilities allow me to move back and forth between realms, the thin filter that separates us from one level of reality to another, as routinely as some of you may go to the corner store. Before I became a doula, I was a medium so I am comfortable communicating with those who have passed and grateful to assist those who yearn to connect with loved ones on Earth. It is a privilege to work with this kind of communication between realms, and being a medium comes into play as I sit bedside as a doula and watch the transformation unfold.

What's the difference between a psychic and a medium?

I am both a psychic and a medium, and I'll describe the difference to you, since they involve different responsibilities and different skills. Just for the record, being a psychic is not the same as being a medium. However, all mediums are psychics but not all psychics are mediums.

Here's the difference. A psychic retrieves information about things like relationships, career, money, love, life path, and health.

In my work as a medium, I reach a higher energetic "vibration" to connect and communicate with those who have passed over. People who are on the other side are able to communicate and send messages through me as a medium to their loved ones on Earth. I'm the vessel, the channel, and it takes extraordinary focus and "tuning in" to receive and pass on these messages. Whenever I'm doing a reading, I always ask Spirit to reveal to me only that information that's for the greatest good.

There's also an important difference between interacting as a medium with those who have passed, and what I see as a medium and death doula sitting bedside with the dying.

As a death doula and medium, I can see that at the end of life our souls are in a place different from the souls of those who have already passed or "crossed over," and you'll see evidence of this in the stories and lessons in the coming pages.

What patients "see" at the end of life

Patients at the end of life are in a place that we can't name, but we know it well. In this place, everyone is engaged in flowing, loving relationships—a constant flow of faces and spirit.

On the way to your journey, your consciousness is prepared

for this new dimension, so unlike our earthly existence. The process of passing allows us to separate what is behind us as we cross the threshold into a realm of higher existence.

At end of life, our souls encounter different experiences along the route, depending on where we are in the process. As a medium and death doula, I see the actively dying on this end-of-life journey, and know they are at the "front end" of the journey and still "en route."

Someone who is actively dying might revisit friends and memories and favorite places. In the process, they become at ease, and when they eventually transition they're already familiar with their new abode and with higher dimensions. Then, once they successfully cross over, they arrive in this new place, their new home. At this point, they're no longer on the journey.

By contrast, as a medium, I communicate with those who have already passed and are beyond the journeying stage. They've reached their destination and have the ability to share how they spend their time and reflect on how they lived their lives on Earth. Their soul's journey on Earth is complete.

In the next part of this book, I'll share with you the journeys and experiences of many hospice patients I sat with in their final days. You'll learn more about their individual souls' journeys, each journey universal but unique, as they move beyond their earthly, physical senses. So join me now on this passage of love that I've had the privilege of witnessing and now share with you.

Part Three

Lesson One: Death is Not About Dying. It's About Living

It's 9:00 am and today's my first day as a death doula. *Can I handle the work? How will I know what to do?*

My stomach is churning and beads of sweat slide off my neck as I think about what I've gotten myself into. *What if a patient dies on me?* I've never been at an in-patient hospice facility before and although as a medium I talk to people who've passed all the time, this is different. These hospice patients are still alive.

This morning, I'm meeting another volunteer who will show me the ropes. I'll spend the morning shadowing my mentor, interacting with patients, and familiarizing myself with the physical layout. Then I'll fly solo. I take a deep breath as it sinks in that soon I'll be on my own.

I'm dressed in black slacks and a white shirt, a silver watch circling my wrist, my hospice badge clipped to my pants pocket. I pull my long dark hair back into a ponytail, and as I eye myself in the mirror, I see a petite woman who looks more confident than she feels. My heart is pounding as I think about the day ahead. I'm not *afraid*. Just nervous. *Will I be any good at this?*

One of the doulas I met in training said her first three patients died on her. After that, she freaked out and decided to volunteer with patients who weren't actively dying. I hope that doesn't happen to me.

I pull into the long driveway leading to the main hospice building and park my car. It's been raining nonstop and I splash through a puddle as I make my way to the facility. The sky is dark even though it's mid-morning. Earlier, I was too nervous to eat breakfast and now my stomach is rumbling. I check my purse to make sure the granola bar I tucked inside is still there. It is.

My hands are clammy as I cross the threshold and open the front door, then continue down the hall to the nursing station, where my mentor is waiting. As I pass through the hall, I take in the artwork, the tribute plaques and the inspirational quotes. The only sound I hear comes from a group of nurses chatting beside the water fountain.

A stylishly dressed man with silver grey hair waves at me. My mentor. I'm surprised. I was expecting a woman. An assumption on my part. But I soon understand the job of a doula is about commitment, not gender, which means anyone can do it.

"Matt," he says, shaking my hand. He nods toward the lounge down the hall, signaling we should move there to chat. As we walk, Matt says he used to be an insurance broker but is now retired and has been a volunteer for three years. He tells me he specifically wanted to be a doula. I breathe a sigh of relief. With his business background, like me, and his shift to a more spiritual way of life, we'll be a good match.

The lounge is a tastefully furnished room with low couches and pale carpet. I take a seat on the tan couch and he sits across from me and explains how he approaches a patient. First, he enters the room and introduces himself, and then says he is going to sit with them. He may touch them on the shoulder for reassurance or stand next to their bed.

I nod along. So far this all makes sense.

He then explains the breathing of hospice patients who are approaching end of life. They may breathe rapidly, he says, and then stop. This is called Cheyne-Stokes breathing. When they stop breathing, he starts counting. Sometimes he counts up to 50, sometimes it's to 100.

"You get used to it," he says, probably in response to the look of panic on my face. Matt says he meditates when he visits the patients, which sounds like a good idea and one I'll definitely consider.

He indicates that he prefers not chatting with the patients, which is why he feels so comfortable sitting with actively dying patients who are not responsive. He is not a talker, preferring to sit quietly and meditate.

Matt pauses, and then admits he wonders if he's really doing anything. Is he accomplishing anything when he sits with these patients, he asks.

I mention another volunteer who asked the same question about her work with pediatric patients. Finally, she concluded she was providing adult support for the nursing staff. I tell Matt I believe he's providing a therapeutic presence—a gift—even if it's not always evident. I feel his calm presence would provide a beneficial impact to the patients, one of the aspects doulas bring to this work.

Matt nods as if considering what I said and then suggests we visit a few patients. We head down the hall to the first patient's room.

My first hospice patient.

The woman in the room is young, probably in her twenties. Her breath is ragged as she sleeps. As I wrinkle my nose, I realize the room smells of plastic and carryout. I don't know what death looks, sounds, or smells like, but there's something about this room that reminds me of my experience with family members at end of life. The young woman is unresponsive, in a comatose state and doesn't appear to even know we've entered the room. I center myself as Matt speaks and touches her gently on her shoulder. She begins to breathe rapidly, then settles back and relaxes.

The room is bare and the television is switched on to the meditation channel. Soft piano music quietly fills the space, providing a peaceful counterpoint to the patient's noisy breathing. It's as if she has finished running a race and is trying to catch her breath. We stay with the patient for only a few minutes as my mentor assures her that she is safe and loved.

From there, we make our way down the hall to see our next patient, a sedated older woman. The large teddy bear on her dresser is the only personal object in her room. The energy in the room is unmistakable: It's the aura of terminal illness.

So far that morning, I met two patients, neither of whom are responsive. *Is this what it will be like?* Somehow I thought there might be more communication. But I can see that the norm is likely to be passivity, and I feel comfortable with that.

I check the patient roster. In contrast to the young woman, this patient is 82 years old and was moved to hospice two days ago. This scenario is a common one, since patients often enter hospice for their last days or weeks.

We don't stay long. Once again, Matt tells the patient she is in a safe place and is loved.

How does he know that? I wonder.

When Matt touches each of these patients on the shoulder, I note they begin to breathe rapidly, almost anxiously.

I tune in for a moment. *Why does their breathing change?* I then "see" Matt is grounding the patients. It is unintentional since Matt doesn't know he is doing that, but it's there. While Matt thinks he is reassuring these patients, the reality is that by touching them, he is physically connecting his lower energy to their higher vibration, and unintentionally creating an energetic response beyond his "earthly reassurance." The patients are attempting to connect to a higher plane when Matt is touching them, which can produce a somewhat jarring effect for the patient. Through my work as a medium, I know that when a lower vibration connects with a higher one, it can have a grounding effect. That appears to be what is happening with these two women.

I make a mental note not to touch the patients until I know more about this work as a doula and I see how other patients react.

A nurse enters the room while Matt and I visit this patient. "There's an angry patient in another room who's demanding to go outside," she says. She glances at me and adds, "Patients are only allowed outside with supervision." She apologizes for the patient's behavior and says to prepare ourselves.

Assuring her we'll head there immediately, we start down the hall, passing orderlies and aides carrying trays of food to patients. I wonder what will happen next. Will the patient order us to leave? Will she be hysterical? I'm acutely aware that I don't have any counseling training and this will be trial by fire. I shudder as I think about what I've gotten myself into.

Another young patient

Before entering this patient's room with Matt, I take a deep breath, center myself, and think about how I can best be of service. But as soon as I'm inside the room, I feel comfortable and relax. She and I have a wordless connection. *I can do this*, I think.

The patient, Candace, a 30-year-old woman, wears a violet knitted cap on her completely bald head. She's lost her eyebrows and eyelashes too. She looks vulnerable and so very young. She's in a hospital gown and the back gapes open as she moves about the room. The patient is crying, twisting the ties on her hospital gown round and round her fingers as she sobs. Her face is puffy, and I assume she must be on steroids. The young woman is ambulatory, meaning she's able to walk, carry on a conversation, feed herself, and participate in activities. Yet she's in hospice. Patients sometimes enter hospice, are discharged and don't come back for months, sometimes even longer. It happens. Maybe it will happen with this patient.

We chat for a couple of minutes and I mention that I like her nail polish, which is a shade of lilac. Candace brightens when I say the color reminds me of a beautiful lilac bush.

There's a stack of adult coloring books on her dresser and we chat about them. Using these coloring books is meant to be a relaxing and stress-relieving activity for her—and other patients. I ask how she likes them as Matt listens in.

"I've been coloring in them every day," she says. "Sometimes it's the only thing I do."

Candace continues crying as she talks about her books and her nail polish. This reminds me of an encounter I might have with someone at a beauty salon, except this woman is bald, crying and in a hospital gown in hospice.

I notice then that everything in her room is violet. The color of Spirit. I wonder if the patient picked it out on purpose or if it just happened that way. I note the violet headrest, a violet notebook, even her hospital gown is violet. No matter how it happened, I have a feeling it's not a coincidence.

Candace says she'd like to go outside, so the three of us make our way to her private patio, accessible through the French doors on the side of her room. The patio is landscaped with flowering trees and looks peaceful and welcoming.

"Would you like company," I ask.

She shakes her head.

That's her prerogative, but we still have to be with her since patients can't be outside on their own. I walk behind her and close the flap on her gown as she makes her way to one of the two Chippendale benches facing each other. She takes a seat and places her coloring books and bag of colored pencils beside her.

It's stopped raining, so Matt and I position our chairs to take full advantage of the sunshine. On the patio it's still and hot, and all around us birds are chirping.

I watch as Candace chooses her pencils. She colors quietly, and even though it's peaceful, tears stream down her face. Every once in a while, she twists the ties of her gown and continues coloring.

As I observe her, I feel a strange sensation in my chest. A sort of pang. Grief. That's what I'm feeling. After a while, I walk over and stand next to her. She looks up as if she's wondering what I'm doing there.

"Do you need anything?" I ask.

"No," she says and looks back down at her coloring book.

I glance at her work and see images of mandalas and sacred geometry colored in soft lilacs, delicate pinks, bright reds—the colors of the chakras. What she's done is intricate and seems to help her enter into a meditative state. At least she's stopped crying for now.

An hour later, the nurse returns to say we're needed elsewhere. This brings the patient to tears again as her brief stay outdoors is over. Since it appeared to do her so much good, I'm desperate to keep her outside. I try to think of a way to keep her out in the sunshine and ask the nurse if we can leave her on the bench on her patio.

The nurse shakes her head. "No, someone needs to stay with her."

Hospice looks so homey, but I also realize it's a medical facility with rules and regulations that we must adhere to.

I speak to the patient for a few more minutes. Matt does not speak, partially to make way for me to do the initial interaction, and partly because he sees I have a sense of this patient, so I lead the way.

We chat about her coloring, the blossoms on the flowering shrubs. I let her lead the conversation and she tells me she'll be going home in a few days.

"I bet you're looking forward to that," I say.

She nods. "But I'm anxious, too. Sorting things out is complicated."

"What would be helpful?" I ask.

With a shrug she says, "I'm not sure. Support, I suppose."

I ask her about her family and friends and make a few suggestions, including therapeutic support. She uses her colored pencil to make notes. When we finish, she seems calmer and has stopped crying—at least for now.

As Matt and I leave, I think about how talking with her seemed to help, at least for the moment. I hope it relaxed her too. Her attitude seems to have shifted and I hope it will stay that way for awhile. I'm sorry we have to leave, and say that I'll stop by and visit. She surprises me when she reaches out and I feel her soft hand press against mine.

Sacred Reflections

This patient brings to mind a book I recently enjoyed, *The Love Song of Miss Queenie Hennessy*, the story of a woman dying in hospice, and how small but pivotal moments change her life.

> Queenie Hennessy: *I am here to die.*
> Sister Mary Inconnue: *Pardon me but you are here to live until you die. There is a significant difference.*

When we first entered her room, Candace was shut down. She was no doubt thinking about dying and probably feeling isolated and angry. As she colored and became engaged though, she seemed to move beyond this, at least momentarily. And as we conversed, her mind seemed to get off her troubles. She was no longer just a hospice patient. She was someone who mattered.

Providing support for others, no matter where they are in their lives, can be life affirming and bring immense comfort. Those who feel isolated receive the message that they count, that someone took the time to care about them and they haven't been forgotten. They're not just some hospice patient who's waiting to die, but someone alive and worthy. It's important for each of us to make an effort for others to feel seen. While I was prepared to be a doula and deal with death, it didn't occur to me that this work was also about life.

Death teaches us many things: about the meaning of human existence; the importance of being present; and to take the time to care. And to get the most out of life and relationships through kindness, understanding, and compassion. I realized here, with my initial interaction with a patient, that dying is a time to reaffirm and restate life.

Lesson Two: Death is a Process Involving Body and Soul

A few days after my first day shadowing Matt, I'm back for my morning shift at 9:00am. A stream of visitors follows me in the front door, carrying heart-shaped balloons and two mixed bouquets. I wonder if they're on their way to visit a loved one, or perhaps a coworker or someone from their book group or church.

I push the wide doors open, take a deep breath and remind myself that I can do this.

Today I'll start out with Matt, but after a half hour, we'll split up. As I think about being on my own, I clear my mind and tell myself to relax. First I check in at the nursing station where I'm handed a roster with a list of patients who need a doula today. I notice the young woman from my first visit is no longer a patient and should be home by now. Next, I check the wall schedule, and see that five patients are marked with purple triangles next to their names, indicating they need a doula. It's going to be a busy morning.

A number of patients from my last visit have passed—a 72-year-old man with a stroke, the 80-year-old woman with heart disease, and the 35-year-old woman with cancer. They've all died since my last visit two days ago. This is part of hospice, but I don't think I'll ever really get used to it.

I check my watch, 9:05am. Matt is waiting. As I make my way down the hall, I pass the chaplain.

"Can I help you?" she asks, probably thinking I'm a family member looking for a patient's room.

"I'm a doula," I say. She thanks me for being of service and hands me her card. Further down the hall, I spot Matt, and when I join him, he indicates that we should head to the room of our first patient. He knocks gently on the door and a man looks up from a chair he's pulled up next to the bed and gestures for us to come in. He identifies himself as the patient's husband.

I'm struck once again by this patient's relative youth. She's only 61. Eighty and ninety seem old to me. But 61? Entering the room of a 61 year old, I can't help but think that this could be one of my friends. As I check her birthdate, I wonder if she's a grandmother. Is she newly retired? Did she have plans to take a big trip or celebrate an important anniversary?

I know I'm not alone in seeing sixty as young these days. What people call a good, long life keeps edging up and nowhere is it more evident than by reading the daily patient rosters at hospice, where you frequently see birthdates in the early 1900s.

The patient is on her back and seems comfortable as she snores gently. Her mouth is slightly open and she looks like she is sleeping. She has an IV attached to her hand.

Matt speaks to her quietly and her husband says we don't need to stay. We wish him and the patient well, and quietly leave. We don't want to intrude.

Outside the patient's room Matt suggests we split up and meet back at the nursing station at noon.

I agree, and consult the chart for my next patient, all the while wondering if I can do this on my own.

My first patient

I'm on my way to the room of a man born in 1925. He is 93 years old. I knock lightly on the door and take a deep breath as I enter.

"Hello, Mr. Brooks, I'm a volunteer. My name is Debra," I say, thinking of how Matt introduces himself. "May I join you for a few minutes?"

Not expecting a response, I enter the room where a woman sits next to the bed, and step closer. The patient is prone, his pallor is grey, his breathing is raspy, and his eyes are rolled back in his head. He has a gastric tube snaking out of his nose, and a breathing machine in the corner whirs as he gasps for breath. I'm initially taken aback and slowly begin to back out of the room.

At some point, I stop. *I'm here to do this work. I can do this.* Slowly my blood pressure and heart rate return to normal, and I move closer.

The young woman holds Mr. Brooks' hand and pushes his thick grey hair off his forehead. She tells me she's the patient's niece, Roberta.

I check the roster. He's been here 23 days, a long time to be in hospice.

She says a number of family members in their large, extended family have been visiting the patient, but today, she is the only visitor. The room is filled with *People* magazines, old newspapers, wrappers from Starbucks, and containers for protein shakes.

I watch her uncle rub the sheets between his fingers, which I learned in doula training is a common end-of-life movement and sign of impending death. I approach the patient's bed and lay my hand on his and feel his energy running thinly through his body.

Since it's a beautiful day, I ask if I may open the door to allow fresh air to enter the patient's room.

"Of course," Roberta says.

I swing the doors open and hear the sounds of chirping birds. Then I move across the room and stand beside the patient's bed and begin to speak softly to him. He stops breathing. I start counting and get up to 20. Then he begins breathing again.

As I stand beside the bed, the niece says her uncle's had multiple hospitalizations, surgeries, and numerous chilling events over the past three years. Cancer. Kidney disease. A heart attack. Any one of these could have killed him. Each time the family thought they lost him, but he came back.

"We thought he was gone at least three times," she says.

As these things go with the extended process of dying, families are often called to the hospital repeatedly, to be told that a loved one is dying. A friend once told me, "This can go on a long time."

When my friend first mentioned this, I thought he had it wrong. Not having any experience with death and dying, I assumed that when the hospital said, "Come quickly," death could happen at any moment. But I've since learned that yes, sometimes death occurs rapidly, but the process of dying can also go on for a long time. In this case, Mr. Brooks' body was declining, but his soul wasn't ready to leave yet. It's a mystery how it unfolds, but it's clear the process takes place in its own time.

Roberta tells me to make myself comfortable and points to a leather chair in the corner. I fall into light conversation with her as I pull up the chair, thoughts of the patient running through my head.

A bag of dark colored urine hangs from the side of his bed, another sign of impending death since his renal output is concentrated. Other signs are evident as well. Fluid in his lungs has made him short of breath and the "rattle" as he breathes resonates through the room, causing the curtains to vibrate.

As I sit, I sense a fuller reality taking place beyond the reality of the room. Another powerful energy also is present. The mingling of the physical and the universal energies that emerge at end of life.

To another dimension

At the same time that the patient is having difficulty breathing and experiencing various physical symptoms of impending death, through my senses I can see his consciousness is traveling to a higher dimension. To the invisible spiritual realms, which I am able to see and experience as he does, as I sit in this room. As a medium, I am open to other realms and frequencies through a completely natural process. Mr. Brooks has no expectations about the future and doesn't consider the past. He is in a space that feels right, perfect, and absolute to him. I watch the scene unfold as I sit quietly.

"He was posted in Africa, Asia and South America as a foreign service officer," his niece says. "He liked South America best but enjoyed all of it."

I nod along as she talks and then the patient begins to communicate telepathically. I'm surprised. Do patients want to connect? I listen as he says:

The most amazing part of this journey is the undeniable pull towards the light... This complete sense of freedom and beauty I'm surrounded by is completely new.

"Is there anything you would like," I ask telepathically. "Anything I can do?"

I want to continue on with this sense of fullness. It is the greatest experience of oneness I've ever felt.

"Are you comfortable?" I ask.

Words can't express the sense of connection I feel with the angels; it's a connection to the depths of my being.

"You are content," I say.

This expansiveness is the most extraordinary thing I've ever experienced and although I was afraid to go, I am complete now.

His diminished, frail appearance lying in his hospital bed is deceiving. We can be easily fooled by the way something looks. But this man is experiencing a complete transformation.

Communication at end of life

Eventually, Roberta packs up her bags to leave. She leans over her uncle and whispers, "I love you," and he sighs and shifts slightly.

When his niece speaks those tender words, "I love you," I notice the patient's eyelids flutter. Her message seems to register.

She tells her uncle she will return tomorrow.

Will he still be here? I wonder.

Physical symptoms at end of life

I speak to Mr. Brooks again and ask if he's all right. Can I get him a blanket? It may not register that he is in a hospital bed, or in hospice, but he knows I'm here. And he's in a place that's creating a version of reality for him.

He doesn't respond.

Mr. Brooks stops and chokes—the death rattle or Cheyne-Stokes breathing. Matt said that if they have enough reflexes to open their mouth and close it, they're not close to death yet. No matter how many times I hear it, though, it's always slightly disconcerting.

I shift in my seat and listen to his breathing. I pick up my warm tea and sip, letting my mind wander back to the doula training class and what they said about the death rattle. Cheyne-Stokes breathing is a pattern made up of progressively deeper, faster breathing followed by a gradual decline or cessation of breathing. The pattern repeats and each cycle usually takes thirty seconds to two minutes. It can be distressing to watch.

People often ask if their loved ones are in pain at these moments. Fortunately, the answer is no. The patients are out of their bodies and involved in a process that transcends what is happening to their physical bodies.

I look at the patient again. He is quiet now and breathing regularly. A clock ticks overhead. For a moment I sit very still, and after a long silence, I put my mug down and adjust the covers on his bed, smoothing them out over his body.

What did he like to do? What was his family like? Was he married? What kind of person was Mr. Brooks? Here I am, sharing the most intimate moments of his life, and I know so little about him. I watch his lips move in and out, expelling air as he shifts in his bed.

"Be at ease," I say. There is no rushing this process. Each person has his or her own plan and we have to be patient as we wait for it to unfold. As time passes, Mr. Brooks alternates between breathing, stopping, and breathing again. I sit quietly, listening to the sounds of the carts in the hall, the voices of the nurses, the occasional whoosh of the vacuum, and the stop and go breathing of the patient.

After a bit, I check my watch. An hour has passed and it is time to move on to the next patient. I stand, straighten my clothes and say goodbye, and then I quietly leave the room. I'm ready to move on as I calmly realize I can do this work.

Sacred Reflections

While we expect a line marking life and death, in reality, death and dying is a process involving the unwinding of the physical body as the soul transitions. There is no line, just as there is no line to mark the limits of the universe.

Death is a time when the soul leaves the body. In reality, no one is going anywhere, we're just shifting from one home to another, passing in and out of exits and entries in a continuous process. This process often takes much longer than anyone expects. Please don't have any expectations since your loved ones need time to do their work. Allow your loved ones the space and provide them with your love and support, something each of us can provide to ensure a "good death." When both the body and the soul are in alignment and have completed their work, it is time.

On my way home, I feel a great stillness and don't want to speak. I switch off the radio and drive home in silence. When I get there, I sit quietly and thank Mr. Brooks for allowing me to be of service. I feel blessed.

Lesson Three: Families of Hospice Patients Need Support, Too

Last night I tossed and turned until 3:00am, before I finally drifted off. I woke groggily at 6:00am thinking I'd overslept, but then showered and dressed for the day. I'll be on my own today. I can do this. *Right?* I think of positive affirmations: *I trust my intuition! I'm ready for whatever comes my way!* I'm not entirely convinced of this but trust that the process is in the hands of something greater than myself.

The last few days have been uncharacteristically cool, but today the sun is out and the air is warm. I head to the countryside and pull into the parking lot, wondering what I'll find. *Will I encounter anxious and worried family members? How many patients have passed since my last visit? How many new patients will there be?*

I ring the doorbell and the woman at the front desk buzzes me in. As I sign in, I hear a familiar voice, and look up and see Matt across the room. He comes over to chat and we make our way up the two sets of steps to the nursing station on the upper level as he tells me there are twenty patient rooms on this floor, a small, quiet sitting room and a comfortable lobby. It's as tasteful and serene as the rest of the facility.

As we chat, a nurse approaches us to mention a patient who probably won't last another hour. Her daughter is with her, but no other relatives are present.

"Can you sit with her daughter?" the nurse asks. "Her mother is fighting hard and doesn't want to leave." She adds that the patient is "guppy breathing," meaning she's breathing with her mouth open.

My heart goes out to the daughter. I can just imagine what she is going through, alone in her mother's room. I was there myself not that long ago.

"Of course," we say simultaneously and then make our way

down the corridor to the patient's room. As Matt walks in, I focus on the situation and try to let go of anything that's not in the moment.

A patient's transition

Everything in the patient's room is lit by the intense glow of fluorescent bulbs. The light bounces off the walls, the tile floor, and the stainless steel medical equipment in the corner of the room. A young woman is standing next to the patient's bed. She's wearing a jean jacket, dark slacks, and an open-collared tan shirt. The light reflects off the gold locket swinging from her neck. She looks like the proverbial soccer mom on her way to pick up her kids after school, not someone waiting for her mother to die at hospice.

As the nurse said, her mother is breathing with her mouth open, a tube snaking out of her nose.

Matt positions himself next to the patient and I stand next to him. He places his hand on the woman's shoulder. As he does this, I flip through the patient roster, scanning the reports. The last sheet contains the list of recent admissions. There are six names, and the list indicates that this patient, Mrs. Rabb, was admitted last night.

We introduce ourselves and the daughter seems relieved that we are there, and that at last, she is no longer alone.

She says her mother had an infection on her neck and is a diabetic. Her mother's experience is not unique. Most patients have multiple medical issues by the time they make it to hospice. Many have complications from which they will never recover.

As she tells us she's close with her mother, I feel my eyes begin to well up. They speak every day, she says, as her voice trails off and her mother breathes hoarsely from her hospital bed.

I clear my throat, then gently place my hand on the patient's arm and feel her energy waning. Matt says he's going to leave, so I move to the other side of the bed to position myself next to the daughter.

As the daughter and I chat, she begins to relax. She tells me she lives in Florida and has two young sons. The family lived on the West Coast for five years but moved to Florida two years ago. She glances at her mother at we chat and her voice drifts away.

These kinds of conversations are commonplace at hospice. It's as if I'm chatting with an old friend, or a new friend, eager to make connections. Everyone is keen to relate here, as if to reassure themselves they are not alone. And perhaps they are eager for others to see their dying loved ones as unique individuals, with full lives not dying bodies at hospice.

As she speaks, I glance over at the patient, who is gulping air. She's now out of her body and traveling, making her way towards a higher dimension. She sees the white light as she slowly makes her way towards it. Her relatives in Spirit are waving and her favorite pets are patiently standing by. I realize she's close to leaving.

I am at ease when I speak to the daughter, even though her mother is agitated throughout the conversation. The daughter cries and reaches for the box of tissues on the side table as she murmurs, "I love you," to her mother.

Agitation at end of life

I've learned agitation is common in patients, and as they near the end, they may experience mood changes and confusion. Agitation is not usually a sign of pain, but it's still a good idea to let the nursing staff know if the patient seems agitated.

If you've had a loved one in hospice for a period of time, you might be distressed by the agitation, even if you've been told about it. But it became clearer when I saw it occur consistently in patients. When I go through the patient notes at the end of every visit, many of the notes left by the volunteers say "agitated," or "sleeping" or "in pain." These notes memorialize the volunteer's visit and provide notes for the next volunteer and staff.

A number of symptoms commonly occur at end of life. Witnessing these for the first time can be frightening and overwhelming. Those involved in end-of-life care soon learn that many, if not most patients encounter these symptoms.

A medical phenomenon exists called terminal agitation. Usually staff members try to medicate it away, but it seems to serve a purpose on the journey to death. This patient, Mrs. Rabb, is not uncomfortable but is definitely hanging on and not yet ready to leave. Her daughter occasionally hovers over her, saying, "I love you," over and over. I excuse myself to let the nurse know about the patient's breathing as the daughter continues to whisper to her mother.

The final moments

The nurse returns to the room to administer medication, Ativan and Diamorphine, to help the patient relax. The daughter asks if it will help her mother's breathing and the nurse says yes. After a few minutes, the patient seems to relax. Then she stops breathing. I feel the pulse pounding in my neck as I begin counting… 50… 75. Mrs. Rabb does this several times and each time I wonder if this is it.

The daughter hovers over her mother saying, "It's okay. I'll be okay. We love you," as the mother alternates between breathing and pausing. Finally, the daughter lays her head on the pillow next to her mother and whispers, "I love you. I'll talk to you every day." She says this over and over. As she says this, I see her mother relaxing.

The daughter pauses and asks how I got involved with hospice. "Was someone you know a patient here?"

I'm not surprised by the question. Most family members are curious why I'm a doula. "No one was a patient here," I say. "My mother passed away fifteen years ago and my experience with hospice made me want to be of service."

I think of how the process at the end seemed so natural and how hospice helped us through. And now I am helping a young woman through her mother's death. It's funny how some things stick in your memory. The daughter nods along as if she understands.

The process of end of life

At this point, I notice Mrs. Rabb has raised her arms over her head. A hospice chaplain once explained this to me, saying, "They all do that when their people come to meet them."

We're constantly getting supernatural help from our divine protectors, and I was to learn, they come out in full force at end of life. It's part of their job. I glance around the room and sense others in Spirit are there. I am not surprised. As a medium, most of those who've passed tell me they were visited by loved ones in Spirit.

While the patient was at first holding on tight, she has now begun to relax, and as her daughter's head rests next to her on the pillow, she stops breathing again and I begin counting. I get up to 100. Her daughter sits down next to the bed and looks at her mother. There's a hush in the room. Then the daughter begins to cry.

When a hospice patient dies

It's like any other Tuesday. Except it isn't.

I remind myself to breathe. After a few seconds, I stand and say I will go get the nurse. I'm freaking out a little but I tell myself to focus. *I can handle this.*

As I walk down the hall, my heels clacking against the wooden floor, I force myself to stay calm as my pulse pounds through my entire body. One moment the patient is breathing and the next moment, she's not. I step into the nursing station and approach the desk. I half expect something dramatic to happen, but the nurse just looks up at me.

I shake my head to clear it and say, "The patient in room 39 just passed."

The nurse turns to the social worker and asks her to come with us to the room.

The three of us make our way back to the patient's room, where the patient is absolutely still, her color mottled, her body already livid. As the nurse listens to the patient's chest with her stethoscope, the daughter quietly sobs beside her mother's body. After a minute, the daughter speaks. "She's gone, isn't she?"

The nurse nods.

The daughter reaches out to me and I feel her hot tears splash against my neck, as her body shakes from waves of grief.

A range of emotions at end of life

This experience is taking place on such sacred and divine ground that I have my own mix of emotions. Gratitude. Sadness. Love. I feel all of these emotions at once and they create a state simultaneously full and depleting. I think about the daughter's last minutes with her mother, as she provided a bridge for her mother to cross.

"I will never forget you," the daughter says to me. "You're an angel."

As I leave, I touch Mrs. Rabb's arm. "Go in peace," I say, seeing that her soul has already left her body and is slowly making its way to the other side.

Sacred Reflections

End of life does not have to be a terrifying or anguished time. It can be filled with love, and an opportunity to nurture and interact with loved ones. But many family members and loved ones find themselves in need of support, and absent that help, the end-of-life process is that much more difficult. In this case, a young woman was left to deal with what were undoubtedly the most profound and intense moments of her life. I was grateful to be of service.

Family members and loved ones of hospice patients may feel depleted and isolated in their grief, especially if they're carrying the burden alone and no one is there to help them.

Our lives are intertwined with our loved ones, and when we lose them, we also lose our center. When somebody dies, it changes the lives of those left behind forever. So this is a time when we often need help the most. But where can people go to find the strength and support to carry on at this stressful time?

Providing emotional support for family members and loved ones can be meaningful, especially if they lack the reserves to take the next steps themselves. Don't worry about getting it right. There are no perfect words or deeds but in this case, every effort counts. Your support can make things a little more bearable for someone who's suffering at a complex time.

Perhaps my presence in this room was happenstance or maybe I was meant to be there. I don't believe in coincidences, and I was struck by how, not that many years ago, a young hospice volunteer helped me when my mother passed, and I, too, called her an angel.

Lesson Four: We Retain Our Senses at End of Life

The days are a bit shorter now and a change of seasons is in the air. My work is moving forward as the light shifts towards the fall and longer nights. I'm learning there is routine to this work. When I reach the facility and say hello to the staff, I usually ask, "Who's close?" meaning, "Who is close to dying?"

Today, as I make my way down the hall to the nurses' station, I spot Matt. He was with a woman this morning who he hadn't expected to still be in hospice, but she is. He again wonders, "Am I really doing anything?" I know he is. He's holding space in his way.

I enter the nurses' station and check the list of patients. Today there are five women and two men who need a doula. When the facility is full, or in their terms, the census is full, we usually find about seven doula patients. Those I sat with last week are gone now. They've all died. Every day I tell myself this is part of the work.

Gripping the roster, I make my way to room sixteen to see a man referred to as "Mr. Buzz," who is close to death and needs a doula. The nurses call him Mr. Buzz because he was a barber and his clients gave him that nickname.

I knock gently on the door, as usual thinking: What will I find? Who will be there? What condition will the patient be in? The light in his room is dim and I move to the darker side. The space is quiet and Mr. Buzz is asleep and peaceful. He's very thin, wears his wedding ring on his right hand and a watch on his left, although he is unconscious and has no need or ability to look at the time.

I've never met Mr. Buzz before and know nothing about him, so I have no prior relationship with him. Yet, here I am, walking into one of the most intimate moments of his life. As soon as I walk through the door, something clicks in and I know what to do. Once I go through the door of a patient's room, something takes over.

Faith paves the way

"Mr. Buzz? I'm a volunteer. My name is Debra. May I sit with you?" I ask. "You rest easy." His breathing picks up and I sense I've agitated him, so I say, "Be comfortable. It's a lovely day today," and his breathing quiets again.

Nothing is out of the ordinary in his room. The TV is on to CNN but the volume is turned off, and the low din of everyday chatter from the nurses in the hallway breaks the silence. They're discussing the mundane topic of the latest trendy restaurant to open in the Inner Harbor, a Mongolian buffet.

The patient's eyes are closed and he periodically sighs. Except for his sighs, he isn't moving. I try to hold energy in the room to add a sense of connection for Mr. Buzz.

As I center myself I slide a wooden chair next to his bed and take a seat. Even without the note on the patient roster that tells me Mr. Buzz is a Baptist, I can see he's a man of faith. His room has two crosses, a Bible, and inspirational sayings—thumbtacked to the wall, on his bulletin board, and over his bed.

I note that Mr. Buzz the barber still has a pretty good head of hair. I also see he seems to be transitioning with calm and grace. There is no agitation, no gasping for breath. Of course, that could have been the case earlier today or this week. The condition of the dying changes day by day, sometimes minute by minute.

As with other patients I sit with, I recognize a perfect world, vivid, yet invisible, unfolding for Mr. Buzz. As they sit bedside with their loved ones, some family members may also have this same experience. They very well might witness scenes from beyond the veil in the rooms of those they love in what is called a "shared death experience."

From what I see, it's as if Mr. Buzz is on a path he knows well and has heard about often. His faith has laid the foundation for his journey. He sees where he is going and recognizes the light and a realm of outstanding beauty and peace. He gazes at it with respect and awe and with determination rather than anxiety, as if he's lived his life well and deals with what lays ahead in a spirit of faith.

What Mr. Buzz "sees" is similar to what I have been told about the afterlife from near-death experiencers. They have related their experiences of a realm of indescribable beauty, calm and peace. A realm where they felt perfect, whole and loved. They too were "in awe," even if they were not religious or spiritual.

Are you comfortable? I wonder, as I sit beside Mr. Buzz.

He answers me telepathically, as if this is natural: *"This is a remarkable and transcendent experience, just as I imagined it would be. What the Bible says is true. I have come home."*

He is the most at peace person I have visited. Granted, it hasn't been all that many, but certain themes are developing. It seems that end of life isn't the time to make a U-turn and become someone else or adopt new beliefs. Whoever we are, whatever our faith, that's what paves the way for our end-of-life experience.

A nurse enters the room to check on the patient. She glances at the patient and then back at me, and then shifts Mr. Buzz to a position on his side. "His breathing is regular," she says.

"Yes, he seems comfortable," I respond.

As she repositions him, I see his reflection in the mirror across the room, his waxy skin and his chest moving slightly, signs of impending death.

The nurse asks if I'd like to take a break. "I'll be here giving him his meds, and changing him."

I nod and walk down the blue-carpeted hallway to the Jewish chapel. I've passed it before and always wondered what it was like. As I stand in the quiet room, I leaf through the messages visitors have left in the tribute book on the side table.

"Fly high with the angels," one man wrote.

A daughter remarked, "Every time I feel the sun beat down on me, I will feel your love."

"Make the angels laugh," another said about her grandmother.

There's no question so many of us believe in something more than what we see and experience through our physical senses. I see it everywhere in this facility; I hear it in the remarks of nurses, staff, and family members. And of course, I see it in my work. I recognize more and more that some greater force is at play here, something that, no matter how much I try to understand it, will always be profoundly just beyond my understanding.

A journey unfolds

When I return to Mr. Buzz's room a few minutes later, the nurse has repositioned him and is putting cream on his face. Patients' faces can become very dry and I often see nurses applying Vaseline or swabbing their mouths.

I was gone only ten minutes, but Mr. Buzz has gone much deeper and now seems to be in a different stage of his transition. He was already close to crossing but now I sense a change. He breathes heavily and raises his hands and turns his head slightly. I move to the side of the bed and say, "Mr. Buzz? It's okay." He stops breathing and then starts up again. I watch the pulse on his neck, his Adam's apple, his chest and stomach rising. I reach across to tuck in the covers over his slight frame.

I notice that after the nurses or aides move the patients, the person often becomes agitated. I believe the patients are traveling and touch brings them back into their bodies and pain, if they have any. The medical staff often read this agitation as a sign of discomfort and often rush to medicate, but I don't think that's what's happening. In hospice, the first response is often to provide additional medication, a consequence of our modern medical system.

Similar to a patient I sat with last week, this man's consciousness is in a tranquil space, beyond which lays a beautiful, peaceful landscape. He seems very much at ease, as if this place is home and he wanders about it freely. In no particular hurry, he stops and rests from time to time. His outward demeanor reflects this as well. Unlike other patients I've been with, he's calm rather than agitated.

What were you like, I wonder. Did you joke with clients? Did you have regular customers who'd been with you for years? Have they visited you in hospice?

Mr. Buzz needs to take some time to process the experience, so he pauses, held in waiting, comfortable in that space. I sit quietly nearby as he moves through his transition. I watch his physical body for any change in his breathing, or signs of distress, but there are none.

Our consciousness seems to know where to go to create this personalized experience as we journey at end of life. It reaches into a specific place and gives us that well-loved, familiar and meaningful experience, unique for each of us. If you're an atheist, your landscape may be a beautiful setting or the route of a memorable trip. If you're religious, you may encounter a cathedral or a sacred icon. It seems this place is familiar and comfortable and when we finally encounter it, we ease right in. This certainly appears to be the case with Mr. Buzz. How does this happen? It is a mystery.

I sense Mr. Buzz's family in Spirit is also in the room and he recognizes that, too. They wait quietly in the corner and the patient is pleased and comforted that they are there. They deepen the meaning of this end-of-life experience for him.

I glance at the clock and my eyes try to focus. 2:38. As the patient gasps for breath, I begin to count. I open a space in the room and sit quietly as he continues his labored breathing. The patient is now "lined up," as if he's awaiting his turn to pass through a door. It's a slow process as each in line before him, others who are also transitioning, is processed. He waits, moving up slowly towards a gate. He does not waver, knowing it will be his time soon. He is patient. His breathing is so shallow I can barely hear him. I lean over and listen carefully and watch his chest and shoulders to make sure he is still there. A large clump of white light floats over his crown chakra. It's concentrated and dense, like a mass of white, cirrocumulus high altitude clouds.

His breathing picks up, as if he sees he has moved forward in line and is aware there is no turning back. He can go only one way, forward. He stops again, waiting his turn. His breathing returns to its quiet stillness. He's peaceful and comfortable, with the white light acting as its own force, traveling and pulling him along. The patient is being swept away, agreeing to go, ready to get on board with the All of everything.

The patient sees he is getting ready to step over the threshold. His breathing picks up. Little life is left in his physical body. He does not move, his mouth is open, he barely breathes. The only indication he's still alive is the slightest movement of his chest. I silently open a quiet space and hope this helps. He groans slightly, almost as a connection to still being attached to this plane.

A nurse peeks in to say his family members are on their way. She gives me a polite nod then whisks out of the room, leaving me alone, pulling the door closed behind her.

The patient continues to breathe heavily. After a few minutes, I leave the room to tell the nurse that his breathing has become even more labored.

A family visit

The nurse returns to the patient's room. I watch her give him Dilaudin and Ativan, two drugs they routinely give.

"The patient's son usually comes in after work at 4:00 pm, but today he'll be arriving early, at 3:30," she says to me. She then speaks directly to Mr. Buzz. "That's in half an hour."

She asks if the patient was moaning. "This morning his brow was furrowed and he kept raising his shoulders. It's good he's not doing that now," she says. She swabs his mouth and even though he's not responsive, she tells him his son will be coming soon.

She thanks me for being there, which leads me to remark that some of the volunteers wonder if they are doing anything.

"You are the eyes and ears of the nurses when we can't be there. One of the family's fears is that the patient will be left alone to die, so just being there is a service volunteers provide," she says as she finishes up.

Mr. Buzz seems a bit more comfortable after his meds. His breathing is still dry and raspy but he's not raising his shoulders or moaning. His family members in Spirit watch and say, "*This is what we do. We keep the connections alive.*" There're quite a few of them in the room. Luckily they don't take up much space.

I think of the patients I sat with who have now passed and wonder if their spirits are hovering over us. I can almost feel their presence as I sit with Mr. Buzz. He stops breathing again and I begin to count. I get up to 40. Whenever he stops breathing, I see him floating away, slowly moving and advancing, then stopping to catch up after his work of transitioning.

And now his aura looks like a 10,000 watt light bulb illuminating the room, extending upwards to the heavens. The light is intense and beyond bright. Mr. Buzz seems to be slowly getting his body assembled, as if he is packing his bags for a long journey. That metaphor of the journey was something I would see over and over with these patients as they get ready to leave. You might take your time because you think of other things you want to include or throw in at the last minute.

Go in peace, I say to myself as I listen to his low breathing. He stops a few times, and then sighs and breathes quietly again. His relatives are positioned around him. Most of his consciousness has left and now he is already in the astral realm. He seems to be cruising along and continues to breathe softly but is not ready to leave yet. He must be waiting for his son. I check my watch. 3:15. Fifteen minutes more until his son arrives.

Mr. Buzz stops breathing and I watch him moving away, barely in his body and breathing lightly. He stops breathing and starts again. But now I can't hear him breathing. My head is starting to pound as I see him move, but not breathe, at the count of 39.

He is getting ready to go. He gasps, then doesn't utter another sound. He's gone. He passed at 3:20. Ten minutes before his son was due to arrive.

It's as if Source called him back, which I believe it did.

The temperature in the room drops and I shiver and pull my jacket close over my shoulders as I sense a sacred energy that wasn't present a moment ago. I take a deep breath and pause to acknowledge Mr. Buzz, then slowly stand and get ready to head to the nurses' station to let them know the patient has passed.

Freshly out of his body, Mr. Buzz's ancestors are lining up for him in the afterlife. The patient is slowly transitioning to the other side. Once you cross the threshold, you aren't immediately in your final place. You acclimate and get processed, kind of like passport control but much more lovely.

After the nurse comes in to tend to the body, I slip into the lounge and sit quietly. With Mr. Buzz's death, I witnessed the veil between the worlds opening and the special grace and magnitude of that. I am deeply affected by what I have witnessed. It's not a loss. It's whole and perfect but I feel drained.

I need a ritual. I close my eyes and wish the patient grace and ease. I thank him for the opportunity to serve as I hold a calm space in his honor.

When I get home, I light a candle and say a prayer, then run a bath with salts to clear the energy from my body. We pick up energy from others all the time but especially at hospice, where there are so many different energies, from ill patients to distressed family members to busy clinicians and, finally, to the dying. We need a way to release them. These energies need to be honored as well as cleared, as we move forward.

Sacred Reflections

Even if they appear unresponsive, patients are aware of what's going on at end of life. They know if someone has walked in or out of the room; they can still hear and register information.

Patients appear to integrate this external information into their end-of-life process and are aware of larger physical realities that exist. They're able to register conversations, even days and dates. Anecdotal evidence suggests it's common for patients to interact with their environment even up to the moment of death. I have witnessed this quite often at hospice.

Mr. Buzz passed ten minutes before his son was due to arrive for his daily visit. *Coincidence?* Mr. Buzz's passing showed me he was certainly aware of time, even though he obviously couldn't see a clock or keep tabs on the time of day.

While the decision to pass may seem arbitrary, many patients hang on until someone arrives, or if they want privacy, they pass right before or after loved ones are scheduled to arrive or shortly after they leave. Patients seem to sense this timing and make decisions around it, suggesting there is much more to the mind-body connection than we know. Even though the patients may be in an altered state, their senses appear to be intact.

If end of life and death is a continuation, not an end as so many believe, then this show of free will at the moment of death seems to confirm the independent nature of our consciousness and its lack of absolute reliance on the physical body.

How should we evaluate death and end of life? Through the lens of science? Through the metaphysical? Or is it just beyond or between us, with complexities that far exceed our beliefs?

Lesson Five: It's Impossible to Predict When Death Will Occur

Over the next month I begin to feel as if I belong, as if I'm part of a community, something larger than myself. It feels good, particularly since I'm a naturally shy person, unless I'm onstage. Mostly I lay low and want to show that I'm here for the long haul. I'm happy to help out and even ask to lend a hand with the grunt work, like clearing trays or tossing out flowers.

This morning, it's quiet as I make my way up the drive. Deer graze on the hillside, and farther ahead, I see a flock of geese. I proceed up the hill and look back and spot a fox in the meadow below. I think he sees me, too, because he makes his way to a grove of trees and disappears.

I wonder what's ahead today. Will it be quiet? Will I encounter something I haven't experienced before? Will I be able to handle it? I'm still new at this. Still figuring it out. When I walk into a patient's room, I always pray I can do the work.

After I park my car, I walk past the stone path, through the garden. When I enter the building, I say hello to the usual volunteers at the front desk. They wave back at me as I head to the nursing station, where three nurses are drinking coffee out of plastic cups while they chat about their patients. I quickly think back to the investment business when I use to manage money. The nurses' station here is a complete 180 degrees from money management. Death and finance don't really have much in common.

Today, there are Mars bars and Famous Amos cookies in a bowl on the counter. These people constantly haul in cookies, cakes, leftover desserts, all kinds of goodies. I look at the Mars bars and debate whether I should have one. I restrain myself and glance at the board with the list of patients. Then I decide to go to my happy place and pick up a chocolate chip cookie on my way out, reminding myself chocolate is an antioxidant. Today six patients, born between 1921 and 1964, need a doula. A nurse says one of the patients has family with them, so I make my way to another patient. Mrs. Jones, born April 2, 1953, who has a purple triangle next to her name so I know she needs a doula.

I knock softly on Mrs. Jones' door and center myself. As I enter the room, I notice the patient is on her back with her mouth open. A man is sitting in the corner of the room. He smiles as I walk in and says hello as I make my way to the patient's bed.

The patient is very quiet, not moving her arms and breathing lightly. It's almost as if she is engrossed in something and not to be disturbed. Pictures of water flowing over rocks and mountain streams are broadcast from the TV, which is tuned to the meditation channel, which is on in most of the doula patient rooms.

I introduce myself to the man—her son—and explain what I do. He thanks me for being there. As I stand beside the patient, I survey her room, which is jam-packed with plants and flowers, pictures of family and a scroll of the Ten Commandments. I check the roster and under religion it indicates she's a Catholic. An oxygen tank sits in a corner of the room. The room has a nice feel to it, except that the occupant, Mrs. Jones, is prone on the bed breathing deeply. She does not appear agitated but it could be that she is heavily sedated. She snores slightly.

I introduce myself to the patient even though she is not responsive. "Hello, Mrs. Jones. I'm a volunteer. My name is Debra and I'm going to sit with you for a bit. You have some lovely pictures of your family and beautiful flowers in your room," I say, as she continues to snore softly.

The patient seems at peace. A quiet but unbroken energy runs through the room and I feel its steady thrum.

I ask the son if I can get him anything. He doesn't need anything in particular but says he would enjoy some company.

As I take a seat in the chair next to the bed, he begins to tell me about his mother. "My mother smoked for thirty years," he says. "She quit five years ago but developed a cough. We begged her to get it checked out but by the time she did, it was too late. She was so smart but she waited too long. We all feel terribly guilty." As he speaks he picks at an invisible thread on his pants leg.

I tell him not to blame himself.

He wipes his eyes and lowers his head and says, "I guess you're right, but I can't help it. I feel I should have done more."

It's normal to feel this way, I say. I then ask if he's considered consulting a professional for support. Counseling services are available at hospice, and many family members find them especially helpful when dealing with a loved one's declining health.

We sit in silence for a few minutes as he appears to digest this.

After a few minutes, he asks, "How much longer?"

I can't say. None of us can make that call. I've heard doctors and nurses say that a patient has days or hours to live; only to see that person is still there a week later. And others, who seem fine for the present time, pass quickly.

I look around the room and take in the photos. It's obvious someone really cares about this woman. Family members took the time to set up pictures of children and grandchildren, everyone looking happy and joyful, which helps to dispel the clinical setting. Mementos from travel are tucked in the bulletin board, a note from her book club and cards from well-wishers are taped to the mirror. Memories preserved in papers and photos; the visible story of what gave meaning to her life.

A table of drinks — orange juice, lemonade, flavored waters — sits next to her bed, along with swabs to wipe her mouth. The son says the drinks have been sitting there for days. His mother can't drink them and the family doesn't want them.

The patient is non-responsive. I watch her floating in an

etheric realm, engaging with a number of family members who are there for her. She reaches out to touch them, to say hello, and her arm moves up as she seems to be saying she is coming. Her heart chakra is transforming, like a starburst, radiating from a powerful light source. As I watch this occur, the scene appears to me naturally from an open connection as it does when I'm doing a mediumship reading.

The patient herself is becoming light, the white light extending far beyond her physical body. Her head is on the pillow, the covers pulled up to her chin, her consciousness is elsewhere, her face in repose.

I watch the scene as if through a filter. Although these events are occurring in an etheric realm, at the same time I am accessible in the physical realm and continue to observe the patient's vital signs.

A nurse enters to say she is going to give the patient her meds. "For pain and anxiety," she says, as she gathers her supplies and pulls back the plunger on the syringe. The patient tolerates the medicine fine, and continues to breathe quietly.

I look up and the patient is frowning. She stops breathing, but then starts again. She appears to be moving along as I watch her out of body, making her way. Her son sits in the corner of the room, checking his cell phone and staring out across the patio. I pick up my glass of water from the table and pour the son a glass of water, too.

"Are you okay?" I ask him.

"I'm fine," he says. "This is just hard."

A spiritual path through the afterlife

Are you okay, I ask the patient silently.

"*There are beautiful flowers and magnificent light here, unlike anything I've seen before. There's so much more to see, too, more than anywhere I've ever been. My loved ones are doing wonderful things here, so engaged and involved. They are 'right there,'*" as she points ahead of her.

She's picking her way, slowly taking a path, as if she's on a hike or a walk, picking her way around stray branches, spiritual pebbles. She's going higher and higher, moving up as if it were a mountain. Now she is moving up more swiftly. She seems to be at peace with this new space, stopping to take it all in.

Her heart chakra, which represents love and compassion, is full of a kind of light unavailable on earth. We might call this love but that vastly understates its force. Its power stems from sources beyond our understanding, vaster and more boundless than we can know. As I witness this transformation taking place, I'm learning that our chakras know what to do, how to perform in this process. Her heart chakra is locking in, like a space station might lock into a landing pad.

"Do you feel the love?" she asks. *"Love is everywhere here. It's wall to wall although there are no boundaries. It's not the kind of love we experience on earth; the kind of love I have for my husband or family. This is the love of All, the love that fills me up, yet there is still room for more."*

Mrs. Jones seems to be in a higher realm now and is moving to another station as if each station is part of a route, at ease in her process. She walks in this space as if it has always been waiting. This realm is so powerful and strong, and carries messages about the importance of our contributions to the universe and the vibrations we each create as we become one. It is beautiful and overwhelming, and I am awestruck as I watch. It's as if a kaleidoscope is sweeping away the current reality and constructing a new one.

Mrs. Jones participates in this realm with no thought of what she leaves behind. I sit beside her as her son leans back in his chair and crosses his left leg over his right, then absent-mindedly massages his forehead while he talks about his mother and her life as a wife, a volunteer at her church, and a retired schoolteacher. She was a busy lady.

As we know, various traditions have certain beliefs about the afterlife. In Buddhism, life doesn't end but merely goes on in other forms. As I sit bedside, I witness this higher state of rebirth as patients leave their present lives behind. As far as I know, most of these patients aren't Buddhists, yet their experiences suggest the Buddhists and other Eastern traditions got it right.

Soon, the door opens and two women enter. One says she is a niece, that she normally comes at night but wanted to stop by because her grandmother said Mrs. Jones was making terrible noises, as if her breathing was rattling.

I tell her that her aunt seems comfortable now.

The niece approaches her aunt and says, "Hi, Auntie, how you doing?"

The other woman remarks, "She's out of it."

The two agree that whatever kind of breathing their aunt had last night must have resulted from a cold.

"Do you think she'll be here tomorrow?" one asks.

"Have you spoken with her doctors?" I ask. I'm not in a position to answer their question about how much longer their aunt will live. Even the doctor may not be able to provide an answer. I tell them I'll be leaving so they can have some private time with their aunt and her son. I wish them well and silently say a prayer for the patient.

The contrast between the patient's journey through the afterlife and the back and forth with the family might seem striking to most, but the truth is, as a medium, I regularly shift between the physical and the metaphysical realms and these scenarios no longer seem odd or strange to me. I am somewhat used to this experience of the marked difference between the troubles and worries of our world versus the peace and contentment of the higher realms. It is what allows me to do this work and gives me hope when I work with others.

The other patients I visit today have family with them so I fill out the volunteer book to update information on Mrs. Jones before I leave for the day. The book indicates Mrs. Jones has lung cancer. The other notes indicate she was agitated and restless the past few days and even that morning, but now she seems at peace.

In my work, I've seen patients pass quietly. I've also seen families who seem to accept their loss and grief, while some, like Mrs. Jones' son, have difficulty processing it. And, of course, I've observed among those who work here the belief that it's a gift to provide this service.

Later that night, I listen to some quiet piano music, which helps in balancing my energy after these visits. Some days I take a walk in the park, or practice Tai Chi. All of these activities help me find that comforting space that allows me to unwind. This isn't a typical office job and there are special thoughts and emotions following these visits, where both the extraordinary and the ordinary can occur.

Sacred Reflections

When will death occur? As you've seen, it's a difficult question to answer. The dying do not proceed according to schedule or comply with predictions. No matter how often people ask this question at end of life, no one can provide a definitive answer.

Many of us have dealt with the uncertainty around death. We might have had a loved one whose doctors talked in terms of months, but the person passes in hours. Or the opposite is true. Our relative's doctors predict death is imminent, maybe even hours away. Six months later the person is still alive. When doctors or nurses can't answer, they're not being evasive. They simply don't know, or have made predictions in the past, only to find they were far off.

There are signs of impending death that can indicate that it is near. But even then, it's an individual process and these signs aren't always present in every case. Patients can waver between life and death for days or hours. Those who are present may feel as if they are in a state of suspended animation, or feel disconnected or aimless.

When these patients do finally pass, the energy in the room may shift and it may become cooler. There have been reports of clocks stopping, butterflies appearing, or other physical experiences like light filling the room.

Some like to sit quietly with the body at death. Others may feel as if they need to make arrangements immediately. If there are customs or traditions that are important to you, this may be the time to engage in them. Yet, like everything else surrounding death, it's an individual expression and choice.

Lesson Six: Our Chakras Transform at End of Life

It's a beautiful fall day and the air smells like "back-to-school." As soon as I steer my car through the woods and up the long drive at hospice, I feel myself relax. This place is so tranquil. Is it the souls on their way to a higher dimension? Or the prayer and meditation that goes on here? Whatever it is, I can feel it, whether in the hallways, on the grounds or in the patient rooms.

I was in a peaceful place in my life when I began this work. I'd reached a point where I didn't have a lot of angst over typical life issues—kids, work, or life path. Perhaps I was brought to this work at a particular time when I could feel comfortable and at ease. Perhaps there was a reason it took me years to begin this work.

Today when I check the patient roster, one of the nurses looks up from her desk and says a number of patients on the top floor have family with them so I should check on the patients downstairs. On the way to the downstairs rooms I pass a large aquarium where three angelfish slowly glide around a large plastic plant. Copies of *People* magazine and *Good Housekeeping* are fanned out on a coffee table, and a few potted plants line the windowsill. As I walk down the hallway, I note that almost no one ever adheres to the guidelines posted on the doors saying visitors must be gowned and wear gloves in the patients' rooms.

From what I can see, not many patients need a doula today. It's the first time I've been at hospice when there haven't been triangles and circles next to at least a half-dozen names. As I consider what to do next, a nurse stops me to say that her patient in room forty-one could use my help.

The patient, Mr. Rogers, was born in 1951 and has been here for eight days. As I enter his room, the patient is on his back and is lightly breathing.

"Hello, Mr. Rogers," I say. "I'm a volunteer and I am going to sit with you for a bit. You rest easy, sir."

He is very still except for the slight rise and fall of his chest. Salt and pepper stubble covers his face, and a beard is starting to grow in but is still patchy where it's not growing at all.

I smooth the covers on his bed, turn away and look around his room. On one side are two folding chairs and a larger recliner. I see a more comfortable leather chair on the other side of the room and that's where I sit. This patient's room has double doors that lead to a patio. It's a warm sunny day, even though it's mid-November and soon it will be Thanksgiving.

As I sit, I think of that expression, "If these walls could talk," and wonder, what would they say? There is something these spaces hold, and I feel the abundant energies flowing through these rooms, the span of human emotion these rooms have witnessed. From outward physical appearances, it would seem as if the experiences in each room would be the same. The condition of the patients at this stage varies very little. Yet each room contains a unique scene playing out, the particular journey of each patient, which only they will ever experience.

I turn back to the patient. His chest begins to rise and fall a bit more but he still seems comfortable. I'd never been so aware of breathing before I began working at hospice. Here, being mindful of breathing patterns is a routine part of our work.

The TV is turned on to the meditation channel, and soft piano music, high notes and low chords, fills the room. The patient is not able to watch, although I know he hears the music. There are two books of the Bible on the dresser and, moving quietly, I retrieve the one with a bookmark that catches my eye. I open the page to the yellow marker: *Do not be anxious about anything. The peace of God, will guard your hearts and your minds.*

The patient begins to cough and his breathing becomes more rapid. I put down the Bible and ask, "Are you okay, Mr. Rogers? Breathe easy... there you go," I say softly as his eyes open slightly and his breathing slows a bit.

At this point, I calculate I've sat bedside with the dying for sixty hours. That's 3,600 minutes, 216,000 seconds. At times, this time unfolds glacially, and at other times, it feels monumental.

Some people wonder if the patient knows I'm there. I believe they do. They can still hear, and I believe they are able to understand and relate, even if they can't express it. I feel a silent connection, and as you've seen in the previous lessons, they communicate wordlessly to let me know what they're experiencing. They are open to this and seem interested in relating what they encounter.

Chakra transformation

One of my skills as a medium is my ability to "see" chakras and auras. If you're not familiar with these, according to Eastern traditions, both chakras and auras govern our metaphysical and physical bodies. We have seven chakras (by most counts) that stretch from the base of our spine to the crown of our head, each with its own vibration and specific function. I like to think of our chakras as our energetic "dashboard," a sort of control panel that displays our energetic makeup.

Auras are different from chakras and are considered the "subtle body" or "energy field" that surrounds our human body. Our aura is our indicator that shows how "switched on" we are energetically.

Doing hospice work, I quickly learned that chakras for people at end of life look quite different than chakras and auras for those who are healthy. For most healthy people, chakras and auras are generally shown to me in the form of "information," which might include life path, connection to Spirit, commitment to family and loved ones, and indications of physical conditions. I find that information in the chakras and auras can be used to check on a person's status across a number of fields, physiologic, emotional and spiritual. Our chakras and auras may also contain "light," which indicates an individual's connection to Spirit. But nowhere am I shown chakras and auras that are 100% light filled, except in patients at end of life.

At this moment, the patient's chakras are becoming light-filled, transforming as his energetic body shifts to incorporate higher vibrations. He is leaving behind denser earth energies as the white light of Spirit is incorporated into his etheric body. An abundance of white light (traditionally associated with higher realms and spirituality) surrounds this patient.

I understand a full awakening is taking place. Rather than diminishing at end of life, our chakras or energetic centers transform in a beautiful awakening as they connect to higher realms, a key element of this journey of expansion.

This patient's crown chakra, the highest point of the energetic body, which connects us to consciousness or Spirit, is completely full of white light. Its brilliance attests to its power and the patient's crown chakra is completely overtaken by this light. It's not uncomfortable. In fact, it feels beautiful to him.

In our day-to-day lives, we don't have the luxury to have beautiful white light totally inhabit our crown chakra. Too many other things are going on in our lives to have our spiritual connection comprise 100% of our crown chakra. Yet for hospice patients, this white light is abundant and appears to edge out earthly energies as part of the end-of-life process. It's a good sign since it also demonstrates that our energetic centers are alive with force but now connected to a higher source. We are still "us," but also more powerful and infused with protection and Spirit.

This patient's heart chakra, which represents compassion and love, has also expanded and is full of a universal love with no limits that seems to flow in effortlessly.

What I am shown regarding our chakras at end of life is in line with the great amount of white light that occupies the chakras of NDEr's, which I am able to see when I read for them. These individuals have encountered and incorporated unique energies as a result of their travels to higher dimensions, although they return to earth and continue to live. They, however, do not have as great an amount of white light as those at end of life.

I turn back to the patient and smooth his bedcovers. His chest begins to rise and fall a bit more but he still seems comfortable.

"Are you okay?" I ask.

"Yes, I want to experience this fully. I feel no connection to my physical body but feel perfect."

As I watch quietly, I see now that the patient seems to be visiting relatives in Spirit. They're quiet and respectful but they exude love. It's easy for them, because that's what they're made of.

"You are one of us," they say. *"We are here and will provide you with support beyond anything you've ever known."*

As I watch, I think, *Who would not want to go there?* Our loved ones are always there and patients feel their love. Someone is always with them and they are not alone in passing.

I ask Mr. Rogers if there is anything I can do. "Are you comfortable?"

"Yes," he says. *"I am totally comfortable where I am. This is really the most comfort I've ever experienced."*

We have no vocabulary or context for what is happening here. It's a completely untranslatable experience for anyone on earth. Although the communication I'm having with those who are passing and those in Spirit may seem strange to most, for me, someone who "talks" to the other side, I don't consider it weird.

In fact I recognize that as time passes, the work is going deeper as my experience broadens and more facets of end of life are revealed. It's not dissimilar to my experience with NDEr's; as I delved deeper, more and more was revealed through the experience.

"This is a place I never imagined," the patient continues. *"Like the most comforting blanket that's wrapped around you but you feel*

totally embraced and soothed. I want to stay forever."

Near-death experiencers say their event was ineffable, beyond words. From what I see, these thoughts are echoed by hospice patients.

The White Light

I notice Mr. Rogers sees a white light in the distance that he's attracted to. It's brilliant and beckons but is also patient. This light is in a different realm than anything else he has seen so far.

"I always believed," he says. *"I always knew there was something more although I didn't have a background of faith. I thought my life was meaningful. I always accomplished a lot and was successful. Looking back, that's just a blip of what our existence is really about."*

I lean back in my chair as I consider Mr. Rogers' thoughts, and reflect back on my life years ago. Twenty years ago, I lived a high profile life. There's an emotional component to my work these days that's simply not available when you're working for a financial firm.

My work now directly impacts other human beings, unlike working in finance where you can work extra hard and the end result is more money in somebody's pocket. For me these days, satisfaction comes from helping others. I know I can sleep well if I make someone's life a little better.

There's a knock at the door and a young woman enters. She tells me she's Mr. Rogers' niece and has come to visit. I say her uncle is resting comfortably, and as we sit together, I listen to the sounds of the unit settling in for the evening. The medication cart moves down the hall, the aides gather the last of the trays of food. I ask the niece if she'd like some private time with her uncle and she nods, so I quietly leave to fill out paperwork for the day. I wish the niece and the patient peace and send love to both of them.

Later, when I sign out, I don't see a diagnosis for the patient but the notes say he is "very pleasant and anxious." Today he isn't anxious. Today he is comfortable and at ease.

Sacred Reflections

An energetic transformation occurs at end of life as our chakras take on universal qualities. It's part of the shift that takes place as patients feel sustained and loved in this higher realm. As we ascend, our consciousness expands, which is reflected in our energetic centers, particularly our crown and heart chakras, two of our metaphysical chakras.

At end of life, we incorporate the universal truths that transcend the physical plane. This appears to be "standard," and is both natural and eternal. It seems to be part of the larger plan I've witnessed in room after room. Although I don't know who or what regulates this, I can tell you it's a largely energetic process, and that no matter what we do, it's primed and waiting.

Certainly, many religions and belief systems consider death a spiritual awakening. While we buy into the "truth" that life is linear, the transformation in our chakras suggests that's not what this process is all about. In fact, the transformation suggests that the first part of our "lives" is linear while what lies beyond is free and unlimited.

The more I'm involved in my work as a doula, and medium, the more I see how other realities exist and how our life on earth is a very slight part of a much larger reality, more powerful and compelling than we can ever imagine.

Lesson Seven: The Soul Leaves the Body to Journey at End of Life

It doesn't take long for me to relax into a sort of routine at work. By the end of the second month, I start my morning with a cup of tea and a bowl of granola before I settle into a mindfulness meditation. Then I'm in a composed state of mind by the time I arrive for work.

It's quiet at hospice when I arrive. Except for Thanksgiving, this is the first time all the beds aren't filled. The nurses say death holds off for the holidays and others have made that observation as well. When I sign in, the nurse fills me in about Mr. Jenkins, the patient in room sixteen. He's sixty years old, has lost 35 pounds, and can barely walk, she says. Mr. Jenkins was admitted to hospice two weeks ago and already had a lengthy list of health conditions, including diabetes and emphysema.

I make my way to the patient's room and it takes a moment for my eyes to adjust to the figure in bed. Someone applied Vaseline to his face and neck, leaving a sheen on his pallid complexion. The TV pans peaceful meadows and bubbling streams on the ever-present meditation channel. The room's only decoration is a straggly Christmas tree on Mr. Jenkins' dresser, with a few droopy red and green ribbons hanging from its plastic branches. The only sound comes from the whooshing of the respirator in the far corner, a ghostly background for the room's silence.

A nurse enters the room, and asks if I'm family. When I say I'm a volunteer she thanks me for being of service. She administers the patient's medicine through a port in his neck. He doesn't move as he receives his "cocktail" of medications.

I mention the empty beds in the facility.

"It won't stay like this for long," she says. "It could be the holidays. It's also less busy in the middle of the summer. Vacations, holidays—that's usually our slow time," she says.

When she leaves, I pull my chair up next to the patient's bed and check his breathing and the pulse on his neck. He's doing fine.

Mr. Jenkins seems to be visiting a spot on a scenic road, as if he's taking a day trip to a pleasant destination. The scenery is lush and rural, and I see the way is being cleared as he moves forward. He recognizes this setting and passes cafes and shops on his journey. I watch as a flock of starlings swoop into the sky overhead, and Mr. Jenkins gazes up as they pass. He sees serene hillsides, pale blossoms, and senses the quiet hush of the scenery. His journey reminds me of a trip to Charlottesville, Virginia, a scenic but slow drive where you might stop and take a hike or visit one of the many falls in the area.

Through my senses, I see Mr. Jenkins is accompanied by one of his guides. This particular guide, a light being, is there to help the patient move through his end-of-life journey. I'm surprised to see this guide is dressed as a real-life guide, with a guide belt, cap, scarf, tie, badges and whistle cord. This guide has a sense of humor.

I don't always see those on the other side dressed in human form. Sometimes I sense their energy or hear them or they show me signs of particular information they want me to know. This particular guide is playing and that's okay with me.

The effect of Mr. Jenkins' "trip" is one of comfort and enjoyment as he nods and recognizes his favorite spots. I don't see any family with him, just his guide, but he seems to be meeting friends and, like other patients, this path is familiar and relevant to him. These kinds of journeys are common in the days and weeks leading up to end of life. I observe them with most of the patients.

Through these journeys at end of life, I see how a deeper pattern links the people, places and events in life that matter to us, each incident creating a chain of our reality.

The patient's status says "no religion" on the roster, which doesn't surprise me, since he hasn't encountered any religious images on his journey. No churches. No choirs. No religious iconography. He's visiting a place with references within our physical reality. There's nothing random about his journey though, and he recognizes all of these sites. They provide comfort and reassurance—and happiness. It's as if he's floated to this destination on a soft white cloud.

As I sit quietly, I breathe in a mix of cleaning agents, food, and people. These are the varied scents of hospice. As a doula, I deal with them on a daily basis and sometimes carry them home with me after a day at work. Others have occasionally mentioned that I smell like disposable gloves or Band-aids, but I don't notice it.

The patient has now moved on to another setting. It appears to be from his childhood and he is playing outdoors with friends and his sister when his mother calls to him.

"Time to come in," she says.

He doesn't want to stop playing and continues to run after a ball, giggling with his friends. He is happy and content, playing with the children he loves. His mother calls again, reminding him his grandmother is there to visit. He is relaxed and breathing easily as this unfolds. I watch Mr. Jenkins and it strikes me how our earlier life experiences link to later ones. How our beliefs endure and carry us from one reality to the next.

I am reminded of Kahlil Gibran who wrote of this journey through life: *"The most beautiful thing in life is that our souls remain hovering over the places where we once enjoyed ourselves."*

Patients lead the way

Like my work with other hospice patients, my job is to make sure each patient is comfortable, and I take cues from them, allowing things to unfold as they are meant to. I turn the lights down in the room and the natural light allows me to read one of my favorite volumes of poetry by Mary Oliver. I read to myself since doulas don't normally read out loud to patients unless we know for sure there is something they specifically enjoy. The light coming through the slats in the blinds grows dimmer as the afternoon passes.

Later, I close the book and check my watch and see it's 5:00pm, time to move on. I clear away my cup of tea, stand and brush the wrinkles from my skirt. I wish the patient well and hope I was able to bring Mr. Jenkins peace and support. His journey is not like most others I've seen, but then, we're all different, each journey distinct, yet all are meaningful.

Sacred Reflections

At death, our consciousness travels outside our body until it's ready to take up residence in its new home. These travels, or journeys, seem to be common at end of life. They're not visible to most of us on earth, but lucid patients sometimes reference them in extremely real and vivid terms. Perhaps we don't "see" them, because we are not "looking" hard enough or it may be that the links between realities are mostly hidden and only visible to a few. Or perhaps we are focused on this reality to the exclusion of all else?

At end of life, when it appears our loved ones are sleeping, they're actually hard at work making their transition. Their consciousness knows the path for its journey as it connects to universal consciousness, linking to a boundless and limitless dimension. Yet at the same time, the scenery and faces are as familiar and comforting as home, and the travel contains memories and continuity.

For some, this journey may be a time to connect with old friends and family members, and visit familiar settings. For others, the journey brings the enjoyment of reconnecting and experiencing the "highlights" of life. For everyone, though, it appears to be a natural part of the transition process, even for those who are neither spiritual nor religious.

For some who are religious, their journey may involve

religious iconography, such as cathedrals, choirs, or sacred scenery. For those not religious, their journey may represent significant memories and beliefs. Like other parts of end of life, a sense of completeness occurs with these travels. We are able to unpack our lifetime of gifts, yet also take them with us as they endure and become part of our soul's journey.

Lesson Eight: There is Something Larger That Exists and We Are All Part of It

It's a mild day for winter and, so far, we've had balmy temperatures and less than an inch of snow. It's the kind of winter I really enjoy although others might shudder at the thought of January temperatures hovering in the 60s in the Northeast.

As my work in hospice continues, I'm learning there are no "should be's," or expectations about the experience we or our loved ones will have. Each experience is different—every one special and unique.

I fix a protein shake and grab a granola bar as I head to work, then jump in the car and drive north, since I'm going to a different facility today. I've been asked to sit with an actively dying patient whose children have been staying with her for days and need a break. It's an assisted living facility I've not visited before.

I make my way to a peaceful, rural setting in a suburban neighborhood. Four low-rise buildings flank either side of the main building. After parking and going inside, I introduce myself to the two women at the front desk and say I'm there as a doula. They point to a book and ask me to sign in.

"What's the patient's name?" one of the women asks.

I give her the patient's name.

"She just passed," the woman says.

I briefly wonder if the patient chose that time to die, since it was right before her children were scheduled to leave, but before I was due to arrive. Her passing may have been a special moment not to be shared with anyone else, especially someone she'd never met before.

A different kind of visit

I thank the women at the front desk, and as I leave and walk outside into the cool late afternoon air, I blink and "see" the patient's soul slowly drifting up outside the window of the facility. She's in no hurry and isn't in pain. She hovers as if to consider going back in, but knows she's already crossed over. Her perspective allows her to be both outside her body and survey what is beneath her, between worlds. She experiences a newfound sense of permanent freedom and peace, and an expansiveness of being she has never felt before.

Although she watches her children below her, distressed and hugging each other, she is already slightly detached. She's immersed in a sense of fullness, of never having felt that much love before. And of being in the absolutely right place.

I see her experiencing gratitude. She wants to tell her children they will feel better, that their grief will burn, but while it won't die completely, it will diminish. And they will find in that diminishment the intensity of her love and their lasting connection. She's able to express her deepest emotions with clarity and love, not with regrets or grief or pain. Instead, she's grateful for having had the experience of her children and family, and that special feeling that comes from those deep-seated connections available to us on earth.

She floats above the building, enjoying the sensation, feeling at ease. She is sorry her children are intensely in their grief but also experiences a knowing that grief is very brief, a still moment. A moment that you can blink and forget.

Her family in Spirit surrounds her on the other side, allowing her to do whatever she likes. *"Take as much time as you need,"* they say. That is the unusual thing about where she is. There is unlimited time. She has time to delve as deeply and sweetly into any aspect of the universe as she would like.

Her family in Spirit is quietly available and she knows they are there and ready—if she is. She feels their presence; it's like knowing someone you love is always there for you.

She watches as the nurses prepare her physical body. It

means nothing to her. She could have been looking at a piece of furniture. There is no sense of attachment, no sensation of connection. Only a sense of questioning and wondering about this ritual and how mechanical the nurses are, doing the routine they perform on thousands of patients a year.

She watches as her son cries and occasionally asks the nurses a question.

"Was my mother in pain? Is what you're doing disturbing her body? Should we fix her clothing?"

I ask if there is anything I can do for her.

She says she is okay, is in a wondrous place on a remarkable journey where she can breathe and feel totally at one with everything in the most glorious way.

I ask what I should tell people about death. Should they be afraid?

"It is a stillness," she says. "A vastness. It is beauty but beyond beauty, it is completeness and the sense of being one with all creatures and the expansiveness of love." She shows me a large purple amethyst crystal. I'm aware amethyst is one of the most revered stones.

"What does that mean?" I ask.

"It's a link to the spiritual plane," she says.

"Are you comfortable?" I ask.

"More than comfortable. I am filled with the greatest sense of fullness that exists. I am beyond boundless. I am part of the stars and the most beautiful sunsets and the dawn."

"I'm sorry I missed you," I say. "You sound like a remarkable woman. Goodbye," I say as I walk back towards my car, "and Godspeed on your journey. Bring your energy to the universe to merge with the profound energy that exists there. Until we meet again, thank you."

As I drive away, I notice two men arriving at the front entrance, no doubt visiting loved ones. By now it's dark. I see one star in the sky. It is time to leave.

Sacred Reflections

The sense of fullness experienced at end of life comes in full blown when we pass. This sense of being one with the universe occurs as our consciousness merges with universal consciousness.

In my work as a medium I often hear about this state from those who've crossed. They tell me about the unique sense of wholeness and peace they experience on the other side, yet as a hospice death doula, I'm able to see this state from yet another perspective: the perspective of our consciousness opening up to the collective consciousness. At death, we are full of the sense of being one. This patient was able to convey that remarkable state to me as I witnessed her moving to higher realms.

Following her passing, this woman existed between states. She was open and unrestricted but hadn't yet reached her destination. Still, she expressed gratitude and a great love and sense of freedom, a type of spiritual preview of more to come.

I felt a remarkable connection with her and although I didn't have the experience of "sitting" bedside with this woman, I felt we were meant to connect in other ways, as she shared her personal message of spiritual growth with me. Our encounter contains an energy like the links of our intertwining stories. Along our life paths, we are all at different stages of growth, no matter where we intersect to form new connections.

Lesson Nine: Living Well is at the Sacred Center of Life and Death

It's spring and, at last, everything is in bloom. The scent of the season is in the air and summer is right around the corner. In no time at all, the blue jays and cardinals will be back at my bird feeder. This is my favorite time of year.

I take in the landscape that's come to life as I pull up to the facility. I'm struck by how tranquil it seems, at least on the outside. Once inside, the nursing staff and aides crowd the nursing station and volunteers at the front desk point me to the sign-in sheet. Aides push carts stocked with supplies and drinks, while visitors wait in line to check in at the front desk.

I check the patient board and see that today there are seven patients who require a doula. As always, I ask the nurses, "Who is close?" Today, at least four patients require a doula.

I consult my list and see there are three women and one man for me to visit. I start with Mr. Rudowski, the patient in room four, a 68-year-old man. No visitors are in his room, and the patient is on his back in bed, hooked up to a respirator. The machine sounds as if it's doing the breathing for him. Each time he takes a breath, the sound is magnified by a green metal box, with eight dials, two cords and three tubes, one of which is connected to the patient.

Mr. Rudowski doesn't move and only breathes with the help of the machine. His mouth is open and it sounds like he is snoring, except the machine broadcasts each intake of breath. His curled-up hands are stationary. He's puffy, perhaps the result of medication.

His room is decorated with a collage of family pictures of him at a much younger age. One shows his college graduation, and in another he's with a man, possibly his father. Both are seated and wearing matching blue shirts. I see a photo of the patient as a young child, probably around eight years old, feeding a pony.

With the exception of one photo of Mr. Rudowski as a youngster in an iron lung, in all the others he's in a wheelchair. Taken in various locations around the world, the photos show him in high spirits, fully engaged in life. On the other side of the room, photos of Mr. Rudowski's friends and family are tucked into a ribbon board. I'm struck by how happy and involved Mr. Rudowski appears as he smiles for the camera as it captures special shared moments.

The room is decorated with numerous personal mementos. I easily see Mr. Rudowski as a true master of his destiny and an example of the extraordinary potential within all of us.

A small vase of tulips, the red blooms tinged with yellow, sits atop his dresser next to a card that reads: *To See You Smile Makes Life Worthwhile.* A stuffed animal on the dresser looks like the pony in one of the pictures. The TV is on, but the volume is so low I can barely hear the faint sound of gospel music.

This patient's room is alive and a lot of thought has been put into it. This is not the room of someone who is defined by death, but by life and love.

I see Mr. Rudowski traveling to a beautiful farm with rolling fields that go on forever, like the view in some of the photos on the ribbon board. Once again I watch how we use the Divine intelligence within all of us to weave together the seen and the unseen worlds in our end-of-life experience. Mr. Rudowski is comfortable and could stay in this endless and serene setting forever. I also see he is a man who squarely faced the challenges and strife he encountered and chose to live with courage and grace. As he travels in this blissful setting, he approaches the scene with the same purposefulness and acceptance he exhibited in life. Now I'm not saying positive thinking is a cure for everything, but our beliefs are intrinsic to our perception of reality and he appears to be a real life example.

Life taught this patient how to live and how to make peace

with his physical impairments. We are all bound together by love in this life and this love is reflected in a deeper condition at end of life, and when we reach the other side.

An inspirational life

I look up when I hear a knock on the door. A nurse asks if she can come in to give the patient his meds. She moves around the bed and listens to the respirator, and asks if I've heard any unusual noises from the machine.

I haven't, but I tell her I'll let her know if I do.

The nurse then asks if I've read the book about the patient.

"What book?" I ask.

"The inspirational book," the nurse says, pointing to a book on the dresser.

I step over to the dresser, and when I pick up the book I notice one of the chapters has been marked with a piece of yellow paper. I pull it out and begin to read. The chapter was written by the patient and describes how one day as a young child he was running after his baby sister and, the next day, he's unable to walk. This man endured numerous operations over his lifetime. He couldn't write very well but managed to adapt, with a cheerful outlook and determination. He excelled in school, was Vice-President of his Spanish Club, went to college, and after college, got a job with the IRS. When he interviewed for the job, the personnel department asked if he would be able to get to work. Would it be difficult since he needed a wheelchair? He told them it wouldn't be a problem, even though he had no idea how he was going to get there. He eventually took a combination of buses and private transportation.

After retirement this man remained active and had many friends and interests. From his story I gleaned he never viewed himself as a victim, never entitled or special. His tale is a lesson of hope and purpose. I was struck by how this man was severely handicapped yet went on to live a beautiful and complete life.

I continue to witness this patient's philosophy as his end-of-life journey unfolds. I see how he faces this stage like other patients I've sat with. I feel blessed to cross paths with this man, so expert at manifesting godliness, simply through his beliefs which he transforms into reality.

The nurse continues to work on the respirator as I peruse the chapter in the book. Soon a doctor enters the room and checks both Mr. Rudowski's breathing and his feet. Medical staff usually check patients' feet to see if they are cool, a sign of impending death.

As the doctor leaves he wishes me a peaceful day. I thank him for his help and wish him well, too.

I turn back to the patient, who is progressing as his consciousness has moved to a higher realm, moving at a steady rate, not looking back, but continuing on his path to whatever lies ahead. His landscape is becoming deeper, richer, and farther removed from earth. It's marked by loving kindness and he glides in his journey, almost flying gently over the very light but complete vista beneath him.

I am humbled and inspired by this patient who seems to love life every day. Even as he is dying, I can see he's engaged with what is meaningful to him.

Mr. Rudowski apparently cultivated meaning in his life, which is a process many of us find elusive. He intentionally examined the questions: *How should I live? What can I do to live a meaningful life?* He then made conscious choices, one of which was to simply enjoy being alive, being happy and grateful. Despite his handicaps, he built his life around these answers to questions he posed himself; from what I discerned, he made living his beliefs his life's work.

In a few minutes, a man knocks on the door and introduces himself as Roger, a friend of Mr. Rudowski's. He explains he also acts as Mr. Rudowski's advocate, but he's a friend first. They were neighbors, and once Mr. Rudowski retired, he didn't need to pay an aide because Roger came to his house several times a week to help him. Mr. Rudowski couldn't move or walk and even wrote with a stylus in his mouth at that point, but was very determined, and always tried to do everything.

As I watch Mr. Rudowski, I think: *Life really is what you make it.*

Roger remarked how he and the family were grateful for the hospice volunteers who could sit with patients when family and friends needed breaks or were otherwise unavailable. Sensing Roger would like to be alone with his friend, I thank him for being there, and after wishing Mr. Rudowski peace, I leave. Sometimes in this work I make a strong connection with a patient, so although I'm not there when Mr. Rudowski transitions, I know he passed in peace.

Sacred Reflections

When I visit this patient, the song, *In the End*, comes to mind:

How well did I live?
How well did I love?
How well did I learn to let go?

In the end, these three questions are what really matter in life.

While these questions may mean different things to each of us, practicing gratitude for the moment, for the people in my life, for love, for just being, is what I strive to do. I'm not saying that I always get it right but I'm looking for the signposts along the way.

Sitting with this patient taught me to let go of what I can't control, to love with an open heart and to live more fully. All of us are capable of living well, yet not all of us achieve it. And living well is a tricky proposition. It seems as if it should be so easy, but it can be elusive. However, this patient made the decision to live well and continued to live with purpose the rest of his life. It's a remarkable lesson. Not only did he not sweat the small stuff, he didn't seem to sweat anything at all. He was resilient in facing whatever showed up, good or bad. And that attitude carried him through life and end of life. Even at hospice, it's something we don't see often.

Lesson Ten: Our Soul is Intact at End of Life, No Matter What Our Physical Condition Is

We've had nothing but rain and storms for a week so I dress in my rain boots and coat, and wrap a wooly scarf around my neck. With raindrops splashing my windshield, I head to a local bistro to pick up lunch before driving the twenty miles to hospice. I hurry to the door, and when I'm buzzed in I go straight to the nurses' station.

My eyes scan the board as I take a look to see who needs a doula today. The patient roster and the board serve two different purposes. The roster displays columns of information about each of the patients—their birthdate, their religion, their diet, their admittance date and more. The wall chart lists the patients by name and room number and indicates which patients need a doula by the presence of a purple or grey triangle next to their name. So I always look at both the board and the roster, which gives me more information about each patient. Today six patients have purple triangles next to their names. All are women, born between 1921 and 1945. I note a patient I sat with on Tuesday, Justine, is still here, so I decide to stop by her room first.

Seeing patients multiple times allows me to witness their progress. Death takes its time and people seem to have their own process, and like everything else, this unfolding moves at its own pace.

Visitors and family create memories in a patient's room
I make my way down the hall. The cleaning crew is working, and mops and buckets of sudsy water are stationed outside room number one. Two large garbage cans sit on either side of the hallway. I pass them and head to room seven and knock lightly on the door. "Justine, it's Debra," I call as I enter the room. "I'm

the volunteer who was with you on Tuesday."

Justine is in the same position today as she was last Tuesday, propped up in bed on several pillows, her head lolling to the side. Her shoulders move almost imperceptibly as she breathes lightly. A patient call button is on the bed next to her, but I know she'd never be able to use it. Other than her shallow breathing, she doesn't move at all. Justine looks paler than a few days ago, and thinner, if that's possible.

I hear the jarring ring of a cell phone in the hall and move to close the door partway. All the while I know Justine is getting close. I'm surprised she's still here but it's clear she hasn't finished her business yet and is still hanging on.

As I take a seat beside her, I see several guides—beings of light—are with her. As a medium, I am able to see these energetic beings in the invisible realms. I notice that Justine's team of guides have been with her for a very long time, offering protection and spiritual healing. We all have a variety of spirit guides with us during our lifetimes, and they work to assist us on our life paths. Some of these guides are ascended light beings while others may be our ancestors or perhaps were healers during their time on earth. If we tune in, we may recognize their energy and feel them. They are here to support us and provide all sorts of protection and abilities beyond the earthly plane.

In Justine's case, her team appears to have supported her health and assisted in gate-keeping to the spirit world. I acknowledge her guides and they make their presence known with a beam of white light which appears in the room. I am glad to see them here, and their presence brings in a higher energy that is beneficial. They stand silently aside as I sit quietly beside Justine.

Justine's room has no personal effects, only the Styrofoam cups on her patient table, an assortment of swabs and straws, and a box of tissues. Last week there was a book on her nightstand, but it's gone now. It was a memory book, perhaps made by her family in the past or maybe it was created more recently. The book includes pictures of Justine as a young woman, photos of her first car, her children, dated photographs of a man and woman, and wedding pictures—and messages of love.

I wonder what happened to it. Inscribed with comments from family and friends, the memory book provided a wonderful reminder of who Justine was. *We're here for you... I'm thankful you're my friend... I'm counting my blessings and that means you.*

Looking through the book last week touched me, and gave me a way to connect with Justine and learn more about her, as I'm sure it did for other visitors. The messages in the book were also something for the family and loved ones to have following Justine's passing, and it possessed certain permanent qualities since it carried Justine's and others' energies. I watch Justine's body move up and down, but I can't hear her breathing. She's not been conscious or responsive during any of the times I sat with her.

I look around the room and see her brother in Spirit, waiting patiently in the left corner of the room. He says he has been watching and supporting her from the other side for some time.

Our families in Spirit provide support at end of life

"She is able to communicate with us perfectly," the brother says, and reiterates, *"We have a pure connection."* I understand what he's telling me is true, even though Justine has dementia and can't communicate very well on earth.

Despite the dementia that prevented her from communicating on earth, Justine seems perfectly attuned when she connects with the other side. Her inability to communicate well on earth doesn't appear to affect her abilities to express herself normally with those in the spirit world. Once we go to the other side, we are healed, whole and perfect, and our earthly issues disappear. These earthly problems and concerns are not meant to be taken with us. What appears to be a difficulty—physical, emotional, or otherwise—on earth, is love on the other side.

The Roman poet Ovid described it this way: "The burden which is well borne becomes light." So what appears to be a difficulty on earth, is love on the other side. And in Justine's case, as in others, I believe this to be true.

"We support her from our home," Justine's brother says. *"Her cousins, her father, each of us keeps her soul intact and whole. So while she may appear to you as a woman out of touch, she is at one with us. We connect with that part of her that is perfectly alive and healed."*

Would our concept of death be different if we knew we are always perfect in Spirit? And would we think differently about death if we knew that we are whole on the other side no matter what our physical condition is on earth? In my readings as a medium, I communicate with people in Spirit all the time who tell me they're fine, even though they may have suffered various physical and mental ailments on earth. The trauma, the damage, the ordeals, the upsets are all left behind. According to one of the people in Spirit I chatted with, they regard the problems they leave behind as "earth problems."

Messages from the other side

"Is there anything I should know?" I ask the brother.

"You are only seeing a single door open," he says. *"There's a vast eternity beyond that door. A place you can only enter once but the wait is worthwhile. It's the most magnificent and warm realm, unlike any experience on earth."*

Funny, I think. This is what I had been told when I was researching near-death experiences (NDEs). NDEr's always said there was so much more than they could convey, on the other side.

"Should we be afraid?" I ask the brother, as Justine is still and resting comfortably on her side.

"No, you relax when you are embraced by it," he says. *"The pull of those on the other side is so comforting that you will always feel safe. It's like a giant magnet."*

This makes sense since we are energy. Of course, our bond would feel magnetic. Thinking back on my own experiences, I realize there was even a magnetic pull that led me to do this work. And perhaps you have yourself have experienced this feeling of being drawn to something by an inexplicable, invisible force. I think back to a reading when a client told me he was drawn to this work "like a magnet to steel."

"If everyone knew we are here, to make the connections and transition as comfortable as possible, people would let go of their fear," he says.

I eye the patient. *"Are you doing okay?"* I ask as I watch her breathing steadily. She doesn't respond.

The earlier rain is over and the sun streams through the wooden blinds, leaving bright stripes on the polished wood floor. A streak of light flows into the room under the door from the hallway. As I continue to sit quietly, I sense the souls of those I've sat with who've since passed. They seem close by.

I look at the clock and see it's 1:18. The nurse enters the room and says she'll give Justine her medication. She pulls on her gloves and prepares the syringe. It takes only a few minutes for the nurse to clean her hands at the sink and finish the injections. She doesn't linger, but picks up her tray and leaves, pulling the door closed behind her.

A minute or so later, two aides enter the room, dressed in light blue scrubs with sweaters draped over their shoulders. They elevate the bed and take a position on either side of the patient.

"Her right side," one says.

"She's so tiny," the other responds.

They shift her, change her diaper, and clean her. Justine doesn't move or make a sound as they attend to her, murmuring as they work. They smooth out her blanket and lower the bed back in place. I check the clock again. It's 1:31. They have been there for five minutes.

Justine is in a higher dimension than she was two days ago. She's reached a space of great comfort and peace, a point that's remarkable but not unique.

"She is not ready yet," her brother says. *"Her body needs to catch up with her soul."*

I've come to understand a sense of balance must be attained in this process so that both the body and Spirit are in sync as they prepare to move on.

"Is she comfortable?" I ask.

"Very comfortable," he says.

I smooth my low ponytail in place and glance at Justine, who continues to lie on her side, unresponsive. Yet a lot is going on. She's in that special place for those who need to be cared for while they prepare for their journey.

I consult the list of today's patients. Last week I visited a patient in room 37 who is still here. I will drop in on her next.

I say goodbye to Justine, whispering to her to rest easy. Then I say goodbye to her brother and offer my thanks to him.

"Thank you," he says.

Sacred Reflections

We may think that if our physical bodies decline, our souls decline too. Yet, nothing could be further from the truth. Body and soul are two separate things. Repeatedly in my work, I see our physical bodies decline but our souls remain intact and shift at end of life. The decline of the physical body, which is finite, doesn't affect the Spirit which is eternal and undergoes expansion at end of life to take its place in universal consciousness.

Justine reinforced how each of these components is separate from the other. Her soul would eventually make its way to join loved ones on the other side, to live a complete and healed existence. She would remember the decline of her physical body but it would not affect her. It would just be a memory, left behind as part of her experience on earth.

Lesson Eleven: Having Conversations About Death is Important

It's been nine months since I began my work at hospice. I find myself reflecting about that milestone on a day in March so cold I pull out fleece pants and a heavy jacket to wear to work. In some ways, I feel as if I've learned so much, but at other times, it's as if I've barely scratched the surface of this thing called death. It is the most sacred of mysteries, and the more I look into it, the more layered and nuanced it is.

My time at hospice has fallen into a predictable rhythm. When I arrive, I grab a roster to check my assignments. As usual, I make my rounds and sit with the patients—one, two, or three of them. Several patients are marked for a doula visit today so I begin on the first floor, counting the rooms as I pass.

In the first room I ask the man and woman sitting beside the patient's bed if they need anything. When they say they're fine, I move on to the next room.

The door is slightly closed and a woman with short cropped hair stands outside the room.

I introduce myself as a volunteer and she motions for me to go in, and when I do, she follows.

The patient is breathing with a slight rasp but doesn't appear uncomfortable. I notice the TV is tuned to *The Simpsons*, which seems an odd choice at a sacred time, yet when loved ones and friends visit, their preferences and choices still continue.

The woman introduces herself as Frances, the patient's sister.

"I'm so glad you're here!" she says. "We've been worried. Bill has had cardiac issues for years. A few weeks ago, he began to have difficulty breathing and was admitted to hospice last week." She sighs. "He never took care of himself. I guess Bill thought he was going to live forever."

I'm not surprised. Most people do.

"He hated hospitals you know, the tests, the needles." She gestures around the room. "He never wanted any of this. He wouldn't even go to a hospital to visit family or friends. I think he wanted to die at home, but we never discussed it."

As I listen, I notice her brother taking deep breaths, his chest rising and falling under the thin sheets.

Frances picks up her bag and says she's going to take a break. I assure her I'll be there, so she should take her time.

I sit on the chair beside the patient, conscious of the wind rippling on the patio and can almost feel the breeze in the room. I glance at my watch. 2:00 pm.

"I'll be here if you need me," I say to Bill. It feels right to be in this room and, perhaps by holding space, I can be helpful. I think of a loving kindness meditation and focus on that as the patient breathes quietly.

As time progresses, I see Bill has moved on to a quiet space. The universe is saying he is provided for, reassuring him his loved ones are waiting when he is ready. (No pressure, just reassurance.)

Soon, I see Bill going to a "sparkly place," as bright stars surround his crown chakra, and he and the universe begin to merge together. Each of us possesses a small amount of star matter since we're always in perfect alignment with the universe. In death we return to that matter. There is something of the starlight in all of our souls.

Bill's breathing picks up, as if he needs one more burst to get to the finish line. At the same time, he sees a peaceful spot ahead, a large open expanse, where he's going to rest.

"*Can you see it?*" he asks. "*Right over there.*"

I look and see the spot he is referring to, illuminated by an ethereal light, just beyond the horizon.

"*I'm not ready yet,*" he says.

The expanse remains open and calm.

I direct my thoughts to him. *Be at ease. Be gentle with yourself.* I send calming energy into the room and he seems to relax.

I continue with my meditation, which helps to raise the room's vibration as I shift my energy towards higher realms. Later, the patient seems a bit more at ease, and as I prepare to leave, I think about Bill's wish not to die in hospice or any institutionalized setting. Yet here he is. A conversation with his family might have helped him avoid this. I've discovered, however, most patients and their loved ones never have these important conversations, although they have the best of intentions. People are universally fearful of death so most families skirt the topic hoping it will magically take care of itself. It never does.

When I pull out of the lot, relieved to be on my way home, the loving kindness meditation I said earlier loops through my mind as stillness surrounds me.

Sacred Reflections

Most people would rather walk on hot coals than talk about death, but part of dealing with death begins with the recognition of end of life. Since it's relatively rare for families to openly discuss death, options for end of life are generally off limits — taboo. Yet, it's important to have these conversations and make plans about our options. If we don't, we lose control of the outcome.

As I mentioned earlier, approximately 80% of Americans say they'd prefer to die at home, but the majority of us don't manage to fulfill that wish. Home death has advantages, most particularly the belief that dying in the comfort of your own home may result in a more peaceful death. In addition, dying at home may result in less intense grief for loved ones. Being transferred to a hospital can also be uncomfortable for people nearing end of life, so if that can be avoided, it's one less stressor for patients.

Yes, talking about death makes us uneasy, as if we fear talking about our preferences regarding death will somehow make the event happen more quickly. Rationally we know this isn't true, but we still shy away from the discussions, thinking that we're being respectful of our loved ones. Perhaps by engaging in the conversation, we can also begin to view death in a different light. Taking death out of a clinical setting and into the home setting can also provide familiarity and comfort for patients and their families. Opening up the conversation is bound to shift and reduce the amount of stress that family and loved ones experience.

You may find that once you begin to open up the conversation, it's not as hard as you expect. That approaching end of life rationally and with love begins to take the "sting" out of what many expect will be upsetting and difficult.

Lesson Twelve: It's Important to Let Go of Your Expectations of a Person at End of Life

Walking my local 45-minute loop always seems to clear my head, and this morning as I walk, I think about the lessons I've learned at hospice. Death is not what it seems unless we look more closely. As I pick up the pace, I think about how most people rely on the physical sciences for accurate information about death. Yet, I'm learning there is so much more. Each day brings new lessons.

When I return home, I shower and dress and head into my study to retrieve *Being Mortal: Illness, Medicine and What Matters in the End*, by Atul Gawande. It's a book about hospice care and impending death and a follow-up documentary examines how doctors are often remarkably ill-suited, untrained and uncomfortable talking about death with their patients. It's worth reading and I add the book to my bag along with a few granola bars and a bottle of water for the day ahead.

It's raining hard when I arrive at work and I jump out of my car and jog to the front door, following another woman into the lobby. I don't recognize the woman, but she walks with purpose and seems to know where she's going. Perhaps she's a visitor who's been here before.

The nurse at the desk slides the patient roster over to me as I sign in. Out of 41 rooms, seven are unoccupied, a sign of a light day. Three nurses sit at the nurses' station, where a box of chocolate chip cookies, tortilla chips, and salsa are out on the counter. All sorts of food are brought into these facilities and what's left stays behind for staff. Not too many patients have purple or grey triangles today so that means not many are doula patients.

As I go about my duties, I listen to the nurses as they chat about a particular patient who told everyone she wanted to die and had stopped eating, and had even taken to adding water to her urine specimens. The nurse said a doctor was trying to talk her out of it and noted it was a good sign that he'd been in her room for ten minutes and hadn't been kicked out yet.

When a patient is declining or wishes to die, the typical attitude of medical professionals, including nurses, social workers, and case managers, is there is always something more they can do. Medical professionals tend to believe it's their job to do everything possible to keep a patient alive. It is a huge moral dilemma in medicine, where there is always one more test or another medication to try. Not taking the last possible measure is viewed as a "failure."

I ask the nurses if anyone is close today. One says I can sit with the patient in room seven. The patient's son has been with her for days but is now burned out. The patient, Miss Rose, has dementia and has been ill for years and is down to 69 pounds.

"Is she responsive?" I ask.

"No."

"Is she close?"

"One, two, or three days," the nurse says.

I know that having said that, this nurse and others on the medical staff don't really know.

As I move down the hall I say hello to some of the staff and visitors chatting and sipping their morning coffees. I lean against the wall and peruse the roster, and then proceed to room seven. I knock lightly on the door and call out to the patient. I get no response, nor do I expect one, but I always greet the patients, no matter what condition they're in.

I take a deep breath and enter the room. Miss Rose is slumped in the bed. A small handmade quilt with squares in bright blue, hot pink, and vibrant orange is pulled up to her chin. Each square of the quilt has symbols or messages written on it. Somebody has written, "I want to go to Paris." This must be a love quilt designed and stitched by friends and family.

The patient is unmoving, so I edge closer to see if she is breathing. She is. Miss Rose has very little hair, just a few thin wisps around her forehead, along with two vertical blue veins that pop out. Her face is furrowed, as if she is concentrating hard.

"Hello, Miss Rose," I say. "I'm Debra, a volunteer. I'm going to keep you company," I whisper. "Please be comfortable."

The patient does not stir. In the silence I hear a conversation in the hall, where two men discuss their upcoming fishing trip on the Chesapeake Bay.

I turn my attention back to Miss Rose. She's still barely moved, although her hospital gown is slightly drifting up and down over her thin shoulders as she breathes. I adjust her covers and smooth them out over her tiny frame. I touch her hand to feel her energy, which is weak and thin. Her skin feels smooth under my palm.

How long, I wonder? I sit on the edge of the chair and cross my ankles. As I stare at Miss Rose I feel different energies. She's in a silent space and I talk to her quietly, as if she is listening, even knowing advanced dementia has taken her mind away. Her eyes are half open and I believe she is very far away.

I thought it would be hard to sit with these patients in their final hours, but actually it gives me a protective feeling toward these individuals who seem both vulnerable and resilient at the same time.

As I continue being present with Miss Rose, a few women in the hall are talking about food. A safe topic in a facility about death, as is movies, television shows or grandchildren.

"Let's just go out for lunch," one says.

"Okay, let's go to Chili's," the other says. "I'm craving nachos."

Again, it strikes me that these ordinary conversations are going on in the midst of the sacred feeling around death and dying. Yet, as in hospice, there are always separate realities, including the sacred and invisible, surrounding us, although most of us don't feel, recognize or understand them.

An older woman with short blonde hair knocks lightly on the door and enters Miss Rose's room. She introduces herself as a social worker and eyes the patient. "So tiny," she says and moves around the bed as she reads the messages on the quilt. "I want to go to Paris!" she says, smiling. "I love this!"

I agree. It's a nice addition since it's personal, carries energy with it and enhances the energy of the room. Plus you can see the caring of the family and other loved ones behind it.

The social workers here move from room to room, checking on the patients and communicating with the families. Their job is to speak to loved ones and families, but they have to do so quickly since they may not have a second chance. The patients are usually at hospice only a few days before they are discharged and go home. Or they pass.

I wonder aloud why it's so quiet today.

She knocks on the wooden dresser. "Yes, it's usually a zoo here. I'm knocking on wood because I have so much work to do," she says, tucking a strand of hair behind her ear.

I look up at the clock. 1:00pm. I've been sitting with the patient for an hour. She hasn't budged.

A few minutes later two aides enter. The two flank each side of the bed and one consults a chart and says, "Move her to the right side." The patients must be moved periodically so they aren't lying too long in one position.

They raise the bed, shift Miss Rose and adjust the pillows until she is on her right side. "Okay, sweetheart," one of them says as they finish. The patient's bony legs are sticking out from her hospital gown as they reposition her.

"Any moaning?" they ask.

I shake my head. "No, she's been quiet."

Miss Rose doesn't seem to be in pain, but the nurse moves around the bedside to administer pain medication, anyway, pretty much standard protocol. The aides discard their gloves in the wastebasket and leave, moving on to the next room.

I look at the patient again. She is on her side and seems comfortable, breathing with more strength and movement. Her shoulders shift quietly and she jerks her arm.

Who is this person?

It occurs to me that during their final hours and days, dying patients don't resemble the people we love, and we can't expect them to. They are no longer themselves. The parts of them we loved and related to aren't visible to us anymore. They are still there, inside, but what we see is someone slowly losing weight and cognition, and sleeping most of the time. But that's just the physical body. There's a lot more going on.

Still, it's important to let go of expectations of a person at end of life.

Dying patients are transforming, even if we can't see it. These patients still carry their memories and beliefs—and their essence. Readily apparent to us or not, they are still the people with whom we share memories.

The hall had been noisy, but suddenly it's quiet, and combined with the silence in the room, a space opens up as the calm take over.

I see the patient looking up at a nonphysical realm with an unlimited sky. She watches birds, graceful and beautiful, flying freely overhead. She yearns to go to that vast and peaceful place.

She is now eagerly moving up in perfect harmony with that space. She feels at ease and complete. As she moves to merge, it's as if she's supported by soft and welcoming pillows that cushion her, allowing her to sink in and be held in a strong but totally immersive warmth. She is complete.

I normally spend about an hour or two with each patient, but since no other patients need a doula today, I continue to sit with Miss Rose. She is resting comfortably in a space of a higher realm. I watch her, propped up on three pillows, her shoulders moving rhythmically up and down, her arm, small like a child, peeking out from her light blue hospital gown.

I check the roster again. She is 74 and was admitted three days ago. She looks 94.

Soon the time passes, and as I drain my tea and pull on my jacket, I wish the patient grace and peace and quietly leave the room. I will head home and make a pot of tea and clear the energies of the day. I think of all the patients I've sat with, and how their loved ones and friends must adjust to this person they don't recognize anymore at end of life. There are many shifts taking place, not only with the patients, but within ourselves too throughout this unique process. Each of us has an unfolding taking place, a divine expansion that we may not even recognize until a later time.

Sacred Reflections

We are much more than our physical body, yet this is what most of us see and relate to at end of life. The human body is only the outer clothing we wear, nothing more than our exterior that houses a complete soul.

Knowing what to expect when you first see someone at hospice can help us to adjust to the experience and to interact with them. Most of us are unprepared to deal with what death looks like. We expect to see the person we've always loved and who is familiar to us when we visit them at end of life. It can be a shock when they don't look like what we're used to. Where did they go? Who is this other person?

You may not recognize your loved one. Facial expression may change and you sense no one is "home." Their essence may have already moved on, leaving behind a body that seems like an empty container. These changes are a natural part of the end-of-life process, even if it doesn't make the experience any easier. The person you loved is still there, even if their physical body does not resemble what you are used to seeing. It takes a real effort and, of course, conditioning to get used to this. Yet for most of us, who have never been around the dying, this is an almost impossible feat. If they could talk, your loved one would say, "It's all right. I am fine. I am still here."

Lesson Thirteen: Never Assume the Dying Cannot Hear You

Today I arrive at work with a sheet cake I baked for the families and staff at hospice. I decorated the cake with pink hearts and yellow flowers. Perhaps it's a bit juvenile but the sentiment comes directly from my heart. Although the cake is a bit lopsided, the vanilla icing and decorations make up for it, I hope. When I arrive, I place the cake on the counter in the kitchen and scan the cupboards for utensils and plates and set them out.

As I leave the kitchen, a man and a woman arrive. They get busy unpacking plastic containers of chicken salad, coleslaw, potato chips, and rolls. Families often bring groceries and meals to hospice since they spend so much time here and often don't want to leave. I introduce myself and tell them to please help themselves to cake. They thank me and give me a big hug. (Hugs are everywhere in hospice.) The woman says her husband is a patient in room two and I promise to drop by to see him.

I stop at the nurses' station and notice that six patients need a doula today, but as I stop by the first three rooms, family visitors are in each, so I move on. I make my way to room fourteen. Gerald was admitted five days ago. As I enter the room, I notice a copy of *The Washington Post* on the chair. If he had visitors, they must have taken a break and left the paper behind. I knock on the door and say I'll sit with him until his company returns.

Gerald is on his side, resting comfortably. I stand beside the bed and hold his hand; his energy is low but constant. There's an old black and white photo of a young man on the dresser. He's in cap and gown and posed beside a pair of white columns and the card next to the picture reads: *You are my sunshine.*

As I sit down, I see the patient is traveling and reviewing his life. He's visiting a place that looks like Niagara Falls except there are beautiful birds and flowers and compelling light and colors. He's full of awe as he takes in the scenery.

After a few minutes, he begins to communicate with me through our highest senses, even though he is lying still in bed, his eyes closed.

"*I had a great life,*" he says. "*A wonderful family and many blessings. What I always hoped for. But this is magical, too. Do you see this?*"

He would know that I can see where he is and what is going on, so I listen as he continues.

"*There's beauty in every day and we're blessed to have encounters on earth that affect our souls,*" he says. "*Every day is rich and should be celebrated; there's no reason to wait.*"

I nod along as I see he has now entered a higher dimension populated with religious choirs, but larger and more impressive than any we can imagine on earth. He is at one with this dimension, moving beyond himself, as both a participant and a bystander, as if he's waiting for a performance to begin. He knows that he fits perfectly here. He is hovering over the space and melding with it at the same time.

An aide enters the room and says, "I have to reposition him. He's been like this since I walked in at 6:30 this morning."

The aide elevates the bed and flips back the covers. Gerald isn't wearing a hospital gown but a yellow T-shirt and shorts. The aide repositions the breathing tube and covers him back up with blankets. He seems comfortable.

Within minutes, a younger man rushes into the room. "Is he dead?" he asks loudly. "Because the door was closed, and when my mother died, they closed the door."

I wince at his loud voice as he asks that question, but then introduce myself. I tell him that his father is fine.

"I was here this morning," he says breathlessly, "and thought he was dying. I had to leave but a volunteer was here so I felt better. I've been taking care of my father for the last two years. My sister lives in California and hasn't done a thing, but then she never does."

The issue of family dynamics is a sore spot at hospice. Volunteers and staff may hear about dutiful families, estranged families and families who grieve over what "could have or should have" been. End of life is replete with complications and mixed emotions, from tension and conflict to emotional support; to forgiveness and even ambivalence about the dying person. So many issues come up around death. In that respect, it's similar to birth—anyone touched by the new life coming in is changed in some profound way, and death is like that, too.

"It's been terrible," the son continues. "Dad almost died twice," he says as he discusses his father's illness, dementia, past hospitalizations, and now hospice. "My father would never talk about death," he says, "and now, here he is," as he gestures around the room.

He picks up the newspaper and holds it in the air. "Dad read *The Washington Post* every day." Gerald's son kept talking, talking, telling his story. "My father lived in Washington for twenty years by himself but I had to move him down here two years ago because his health was failing. I'm going to cremate him in three days and then have a big celebration. I already talked to a celebrant."

I try not to look shocked, but he's discussing his father's death and Gerald can hear every word. I find it hard to breathe as he keeps going.

"The funeral will be in three days."

I look at the son who stares at his father as if he's never seen him before, and maybe in a sense, that's true.

"It doesn't even look like him anymore," he says, and then turns his attention to me. "What led you to do this work?"

"My mother was a hospice patient," I say, "and this was work I was drawn to."

"I can understand that," he says as his phone rings. "It's my wife," he says as he glances at his screen. "I'll be right back. I have to let her in." He whisks out of the room the same way he whisked in.

I assure him I'll be there, but he probably doesn't hear me. After he's gone I look around the room. At least one person in Spirit is there, the patient's mother.

"We are all here," she says indicating others are present. *"He knows we are here."*

I see other ancestors in the room—great-aunts and great-uncles, grandparents. A whole lineage has shown up for this man.

In a few minutes, the son returns with his wife. As I stand to leave them to spend private time with Gerald, they thank me for being there. As soon as I'm out the door, it's easier to breathe.

Sacred Reflections

Patients at end of life can hear you. It's generally believed that hearing is the first sense we develop and the last one to leave. Since patients at this stage can still process at least some sensory information, we need to consider carefully what we say in their presence.

So, if you have a loved one in hospice, or foresee this in the future, think about the way you approach the person. When you enter the room, announce your presence quietly. If the loved one knows you, your voice may be a comfort. But, take care what you say. Sometimes silence is all that is needed. We can bring peace and calm to the process, allowing the individual to be the most important aspect of the moment.

At hospice I see how families and loved ones are conditioned to believing this is "the end," and their behavior certainly reflects this belief. Yet, if we thought of death as a continuation, not an end, as so many believe, would we communicate with the dying differently? If we thought their senses, including their hearing, were intact, would we react and behave differently in their presence? If we considered dying as another aspect of the journey we all traverse, would our behavior and thoughts towards death shift? And if they did, what would that mean for all of us and what would be the implications for how death is handled today?

Lesson Fourteen: Our Loved Ones in Spirit are Waiting in the Wings at End of Life

When I consider the lessons from my work, I realize there've been lots of personal lessons I didn't consider when I first began. These aren't so much lessons of dying, but lessons of beliefs. Being a doula has shown me how connected we all are, that our lives are inextricably linked. Through caring for others, I realize even more strongly that the lives of others are related to our own. We're all joined together through fibers of interconnection and relationship, and by serving with kindness and mindfulness we can increase our universe's energetic borders.

The day ahead

I see many open parking spaces today so perhaps it will be quiet, I think, as I pull into a spot. I pause at the entrance and take in the landscape, more like spring than winter on this February day. The warm weather tricked the cherry blossoms into an early bloom and daffodils are flowering along the stone path.

Today, seven patients are actively dying and I'm directed to the room of a woman named Rita, born in 1966. The nurse has just been in to check on her but Rita could use a doula to watch, as she is very close.

I knock and introduce myself as a volunteer. "I'll sit with you for a few minutes if that's okay."

Rita is lying on her back. I notice the television screen is lit but blank. As I move closer, I don't see a pulse on her neck. I look to see if her chest moves up and down but there's nothing. Rita is not responsive, but then doula patients often aren't. Still, I see no signs of life. No respiration, and she's not conscious.

I return to the nursing station and tell them Rita has passed, and was gone when I got there.

The nurse accompanies me back to Rita's room, listens to her heart and takes her pulse. Then she simply says, "She's dead."

This is disconcerting. As always, I expect to go into a room to serve, but instead, I discover this patient has died. I can feel my brain trying to process the situation but I can't. Even though I didn't know the patient, a gap has suddenly opened up. There was no gradual transition, no period of anticipation, no explanation of what happened. The unfolding part is missing in this case and there's no way to put the experience in context, even if I can intellectualize it. Perhaps this is a reminder to appreciate life even more than I already believe I do.

As the nurses come in and attend to the body, I send the patient light and love and bid her peace. I stop by the chapel to spend a few minutes in silence in honor of this woman who I interacted with in the most profound of moments.

It's helpful to be able to share these experiences with others, especially those involving the death of a patient. We doulas get together to chat from time to time and share what we do, why we do it, and the joys and difficulties of our work. This work is unlike any other work I've done, and at times it's hard to measure or define or understand. But talking about it with others, especially peers, helps.

As I make my way down the hall, I notice the patient in room twenty-three is alone. Thinking she might like company, I knock gently on her door. As I enter, I smile and say, "Hello, Judy, my name is Debra. Would you like some company? I'm a volunteer." Judy glances up at the ceiling and around the room. She points to the corner and mumbles. Judy is not a doula patient, as she is conscious, has control over her motor skills and can engage. Doula patients are generally non-responsive with a variety of physical end-of-life symptoms.

It's clear that Judy is engaged in a two-way conversation as she mumbles something, waits, and then responds. Occasionally, she lifts her arms and sets them back down. She stares off into space, not seeming to stare at anything that anyone else can see.

I blink and at first all I see is a flash of light. As my eyes adjust, I see her father and a brother in Spirit. Her aunt and her mother are in a corner, along with other family members crowded in. All are in Spirit. Although her family members are very much present, I'm aware they can be gone in an instant.

"You're coming back to us," they say.

The patient mumbles and yawns, then stares at the television, which is turned to the meditation channel showing an image of water lapping up against smooth rocks.

"We're waiting for you," they say. *"We will sing your favorite gospel songs. You take as much time as you need."*

Judy recognizes them from some distant time, some other place, and nods.

What I see and hear in Judy's room is much like what I've seen and heard in so many other patient rooms. The situation in this room reinforces how family members and loved ones in Spirit come in to be with the patients at end of life and provide connectivity between body and soul, between realities we see and those we don't. I am again reminded how our lives and souls travel in one vast, never-ending continuum.

Judy continues to talk.

"What is it?" I ask.

She moves her hand up and down. She's pointing to her family. She sees them.

Spirit teaches me

"This is what we do," her family in Spirit says. *"We send a love that only exists in the universe."*

I smile at that.

"It's a connection from source that only we can access."

I thank them as they continue and Judy watches them. *"These are infusions of love,"* they say, *"and they reach her in all the right places."*

I sense Judy feels those connections.

"How do you know when to come?" I ask.

"Think of us as if we are on speed dial. We're always near so we can materialize right away. It's as if they contact us by pressing a key that's stored in their memory."

Although patients routinely see loved ones in Spirit at end of life, visits from the other side are not limited to the last 24–48 hours. For days or weeks or even months prior to passing, this connection appears to be established and patients may see family or friends in Spirit. Sometimes pets too.

This is an intelligence that transcends our earthly intelligence. It's a space we don't have to find as we near death, because it's already within us. At or near death, we are fully connected to this higher mind.

This is what I witness sitting with those in hospice.

I look at the patient again and straighten her covers, which she has now kicked off. I nod along as she chats and assure her that she is fine. I lay my hand on her shoulder, and as I prepare to leave, I tell her I will see her again soon.

Sacred Reflections

End of life visions are part of the dying process, and according to some studies, these visions help alleviate the fear of dying. These visions have been cited in texts for thousands of years and are well documented across cultures. Not only do they appear to provide comfort and a feeling of peace to the person experiencing them, but they also enable a spiritual connection. Although seldom discussed and even less frequently validated, these visions are not hallucinations. Dismissing them as hallucinations is a shame since this denies something important to the dying individuals experiencing them.

Perhaps an approach that accepts and legitimizes these experiences could shift the narrative around death. If we open the door and accept the existence of an invisible world unfolding at this time, a world meant to help and support us, we would think about death differently. Perhaps we'd view it as an opportunity to experience love and a renewal of our connections.

Lesson Fifteen: Family and Friends May Deal With Death Through Denial

In these parts, as soon as the weather turns warm, people head across the Bay Bridge to the Eastern Shore of Maryland, the most common version of heaven on earth in the Mid-Atlantic. Whatever the reason, today I can park my car wherever I please in the half-empty lot. Then I make my way past the planters filled with ornamental grasses, and wave at a young woman sitting on a bench chatting on her cell phone.

I check the board and eavesdrop on a conversation between the nurses and the aides at the nursing station. Identifying patients by room number, they're talking about what they've done for each patient and who still needs attention. I look at the board and see five patients, all in their 80s and 90s, marked as needing a doula today.

"I turned room six," one aide says.

"How about room twelve?" a nurse asks.

"Not yet. We have to do twelve and then twenty-five," the aide replies.

"Twenty-six is actively dying," the nurse says. "He's very congested but we're not doing anything about it."

"You can go to twenty-seven," she tells me. "She's agitated so if you touch her or talk to her, it needs to be quiet."

That's fine. I'm always quiet.

I make my way to the first room, room twenty-six, and peek in. A woman is sitting next to the bed, reading a magazine. She is the wife, and says she and her husband are both fine.

I go on to room twenty-seven. A man sits quietly beside the patient, watching TV even though the volume is turned down. I introduce myself, and he says he and his wife are fine. The patient is resting comfortably, not agitated now.

I check the other rooms marked for a doula but all of them

have visitors, so I continue down the hall to the last room, number fourteen.

A nurse is in the room, but there are no other visitors. She's massaging Vaseline into the soles of the patient's feet. "You're a doula, right?" she asks.

When I say yes, she says she's seen me around.

"Come on in," the nurse says. "Mr. Angelo's wife was here yesterday, but I don't think she'll be back today." As if confiding in me she adds, "I think she's stopped coming."

The nurse moves efficiently around the bed, adding morphine to a port, Haldol to another, Ativan to a third; the standard narcotics cocktail patients receive at end of life. All of the ports are labeled with masking tape on the patient's arm, which took me by surprise the first time I saw it.

The nurse points to the pulse on his neck. "I look at this and also place my hands on his abdomen to see if he's still breathing," she says. "It's very difficult to get a pulse or even listen to his heart. It's very faint."

I tell her that since he's motionless, it's hard for me to tell if he's still here.

"You and me both," she says. "But he's been doing this for a week. His kidneys have already shut down." She shakes her head as if to say, who knows why he's still here when he's really just hanging on.

But he doesn't seem like he's hanging on. He seems pretty good, not ready to give up yet.

I check the roster. This patient, Mr. Angelo, is 95. Despite being near death, despite his body being nearly shut down, he carries on.

The nurse remarks that he was a General in the Air Force.

That explains it. He is a tough man.

As she finishes with him, I take a look outside at the garden.

As if she can ready my mind, the nurse says, "It's too humid to go outside. With their breathing problems, they can't go out in the summer, but sometimes we push the beds out when it's cooler."

Many patients aren't in any shape to move outside. Or anywhere.

The television is tuned to the meditation channel and soft piano music fills the room with just the right combination of soothing melodies. The patient breathes loudly, almost in time to the music. His mouth is open, his eyes rolled back.

As the nurse leaves, I tell her I will keep watch. I'll check the pulse on his neck and his abdomen, and let her know if there is any change. She smiles at me, exuding a nice warm energy. Without thinking, I return the smile.

Silent communication

I take a seat next to the bed. Mr. Angelo's chest is moving almost imperceptibly.

I see this retired military man as active and engaged in a setting that requires all of his attention. He appears to be "in the zone," as if he's involved in an assignment that no one else can fulfill and he's aware this is his special mission. As if he's waited for this.

"This is better than my most engaging encounters," he says, offering me a quick explanation, although he seems focused on his journey.

"When I started on this path, when I first became ill, my health was failing but I've always been tough, so I kept going. In my tradition, you always do. But then my body said, 'You go on but you'll leave us behind. Take what you've created and go higher, taking what you've learned with you.' My family is always with me and I am with them now. I am busy in this higher realm, not completely in my body or connected to the physical realm anymore."

I eye the patient again. His mouth is open, a breathing tube in his nose. His bushy white eyebrows and white mustache make him look like a mad scientist.

As if he can read my mind, he says, *"This is not death. I am not leaving, I will be right there."* He points to a space beyond the horizon. *"I am going on and will continue."*

Hospice patients at end of life do not consider themselves "gone." They aren't gone, just "over there."

"Why are you still here?" I wonder as a silent question.

"My body's been taught to carry on. So by nature, it's still ticking, even though I have another job to do up there." He points upwards. *"It's how I've been trained."*

I look around the room. There are so many ancestors here, as if they were called to be present. I ask a few questions in my mind to see what advice they have.

"There's nothing to be afraid of," they say. *"Our realm is as real — more real — than what you experience on earth. Real meaning is found in the waves of energy and meaning that exist from our higher level of love and All That Is."*

"Do our souls return to the physical realm in a new body, learning new things each time?" I wonder.

"Your soul is eternal. It can continue to have experiences on earth and with others as a piece of someone else, connected with a higher authority and realm. This is part of our work, serving as a divine connector."

At this point, I hear someone enter the room. It's the nurse returning to check on the patient. She says she has methadone, frequently used for pain, and other medicine for Mr. Angelo.

Just for the record, when I receive information, I am not in what is commonly called a trance state. I can get up and adjust the patient's bedcovers or carry on a conversation. I am connected, very much present and able to navigate both realms at once.

"Is he doing okay?" the nurse asks.

"Yes, he seems very comfortable," I say. "His breathing is regular."

The nurse leans over and says to Mr. Angelo, "I talked to Betty. She says she's not sure if she can come today but said to tell you she loves you."

"His daughter," she whispers to me. "I don't think she wants to be here when he goes."

The nurse thanks me and I say I'm glad to be there.

She leaves, satisfied the patient is comfortable. A few minutes later, the phone rings and I pick it up. It's the patient's daughter. I tell her I'm a volunteer and she begins to tell me about her father, very eager to have someone to talk to.

"First he had a tumor on his back," she says. "Then he fell two times and ended up with 50 stitches. But he's doing better now. You know, he just needs to heal, then he's going home." She pauses. "I don't know why he's here," she says when she picks up her train of thought. She's referring to hospice. "He's not a hospice patient."

Why would she think he isn't a hospice patient? I wonder. *He is clearly dying.* I don't comment. Her information must not be complete. Or perhaps she is in denial.

"I'll visit him when he goes home… in a few days," she says.

"Your father has quite a lot of spirit," I remark, thinking of his multiple operations.

"You noticed?" the daughter asks. "He's always been tough."

The daughter asks if I believe in God and if I pray.

I say I do.

"I can tell you're a spiritual person," she says.

I continue chatting a few more minutes with Mr. Angelo's daughter and offer reassurance that her father is resting comfortably now.

"You're a real sweet person," she says, and ends the call by thanking me for being there.

When I leave, I read the notes about the patient. They say he has metastatic lung cancer, clearly something for which patients are admitted to hospice. They'd likely continue as patients, since the life expectancy for metastatic lung cancer is not long.

I think about the daughter talking about her father being here in hospice only for a short time to get stronger, to get better, and then go home. The absence of the family seems to reveal more about how the family is dealing with this situation than it does about the patient's illness.

On my way home, I drive past the church, the local hospital, and the library. As I think about Mr. Angelo, I'm eager to get home. When I arrive, I don't bother to turn on the lights — the dimness seems right. I run a bath, toss in some salts and ease into the tub. I finally relax knowing my work is also triggering personal growth in my own spiritual journey.

Sacred Reflections

We tend to assume most people want to spend as much time as possible with their loved ones at end of life, knowing time is short. Some hold vigils at the bedside 24/7. But for others, it's an uncomfortable time. Sometimes friends and family don't visit because they don't know what to say. Others don't visit because of their own fear of death and dying. Or it may be distance or other obligations that keep them away.

Sometimes, family and friends process only what they want to believe. Some claim everything will be okay; some deal with death through denial because this is the only way they can cope with the situation. This can be a traumatic, overwhelming time for family members and friends.

It can be puzzling when loved ones insist that everything will be fine. Perhaps they believe that accepting the end is near may actually bring it on. Even though doctors and others may have told them to be prepared, the family seems to not have heard the information or chooses not to hear it.

Many patients also don't want to deal with a terminal diagnosis. Sometimes they know they're dying but choose not to discuss it. For others, it's a time where their own mortality smacks them in the face.

Ultimately, these reactions are okay, because they make sense to the patients or loved ones. It's okay to be scared too—and it's natural. Some people just mask their fear better than others.

Just as the dying go through a process as the stages of their illness progress, family and friends may go through their own stages of acceptance and letting go. This is a time to be kind, not only to the patient, but to ourselves.

I'm not present as a doula to judge, and whatever way patients and families choose to process the situation is acceptable. I just listen and do my best to gratefully be of service.

Lesson Sixteen: You Never Know if That Last Breath is Their Last Breath

Today is May 1 and I've officially been a death doula for ten months. The experience is different than I thought it would be—more spiritual and less physically dramatic. A lot of the time when we doulas are in the room, the patient isn't doing much of anything but breathing. Still, you can't help but feel the presence of something. Regardless, I still believe I've been divinely guided to do this work, and I trust that each time, more will be revealed.

Like other mediums, I can't prove the afterlife exists. But I can offer evidence. The experience of being a doula, sitting bedside with the dying as they wordlessly communicate with me, and their loved ones in Spirit connect with me, reinforces my path, that of having Spirit continue to put this information in front of me. I can't confess to know why. My job is to listen, and when they steer me to the left or right, I try to pay attention and trust.

Sometimes it's personal

Today, I'm not in a hurry, so I stroll down the sidewalk taking in the flowering trees, especially the dogwoods and magnolias with their showy blossoms. Many favorite memories are triggered as I recall the scent of my grandmother's rose garden that seemed to grow untamed in her backyard. It's springtime and already the pace seems easier.

I note five names on the wall chart who need a doula. In a facility of 45 beds, the number of actively dying patients tends to remain stable at between five and seven. I notice Miss Rose, who weighed just 69 pounds but did not seem ready to go, is still here, even though the nurse said she'd pass in one to three days.

I make my way to the nursing station upstairs and introduce myself to the nurses on duty. "Are any of your patients close?"

"Room thirty-four has his wife with him but they might like

some company," one says.

"In room thirty-six, the patient is non-responsive but she doesn't have anyone with her. Maybe you can go there?" the other nurse suggests.

There's a shorthand used in medical facilities these days of identifying patients by room number rather than by name. There's a valid reason for this: Throughout health care, the failure to correctly identify patients and their corresponding clinical care can lead to all sorts of complications including the wrong procedure, the wrong patient, incorrect medication or diagnostic testing errors.

I always think back to a story my aunt once told me. As a young nurse, she entered the room of an elderly patient many years ago:

"Mr. Jones?" she asked.

"Uh-huh," the patient responded.

"I have your medication for you, Mr. Jones."

"Uh-huh," the patient said.

My aunt proceeded to give "Mr. Jones" his medication.

Except this wasn't Mr. Jones. Mr. Jones was actually in another room.

So today, to be safe, room numbers are used rather than names to identify patients.

I make my way to room thirty-six to see Betty, born in 1942. She was admitted three days ago. I knock and call out, "Hello, Betty. I'm a volunteer. May I sit with you?" I slow my breathing as I enter the room. "How are you?"

Tied to Betty's bed frame are three Mylar balloons that say, "Get Well!" They're moving with the current of air in the room. Looking at Betty, I knew she wouldn't be getting well. It's a little bit jarring to see smiley-face balloons and the sentiment attached at a facility where most patients don't get well.

From outside the room I hear the soft slapping of flip-flops on the wooden floor as someone moves down the hall. I look up and notice a woman with blonde hair entering room thirty-eight. I assume she's a family member of the patient.

Betty is on her back, with her shoulders shifting slightly, almost imperceptibly. Her face is blank but they usually are at this stage, when it seems as if nobody's home. Her matted black hair stands up on her forehead. She appears comfortable yet has absolutely no response. I straighten her covers, but she still doesn't move. She continues to snore softly.

As I take a seat next to Betty, a nurse enters the room, says hello and moves to stand by the other side of Betty's bed. "Okay, sweetie," she says to the patient, "I have your pain medicine." She inserts a syringe in the patient's arm, moving efficiently and quietly.

The nurse quickly moves on and I hear her calling out to the next patient, "I have your pain medicine."

Five of Betty's family members from Spirit are with her.

It may seem as if I'm the only one to see loved ones in Spirit in these rooms, but others have these experiences, too. Sometimes friends or loved ones see or sense those from the other side in a patient's room. Other staff, nurses, or aides may also recognize this contact. These are ordinary people having amazing experiences. They aren't channels or mediums, or clairvoyants at a séance. The heightened energy in the room combined with their own sensitivities may allow them to "see" this. They aren't necessarily frightened by it and many find it soothing and remarkable.

I watch those in Spirit lovingly take the patient's hands, guiding and providing a knowing presence. Betty appears comfortable in this process. When she stops breathing, I instinctively lean forward and begin to count. I stop at forty when she begins breathing again. The next time Betty stops breathing, I count to fifty and she begins to breathe. She suddenly stops breathing again and I begin counting, but this time she doesn't start breathing again. I listen and check the pulse on her neck.

The patient hasn't moved or noticeably taken a breath in the last minute. There are no lines on her forehead. Her chest doesn't move. I tap her. No response. I call her name again. No response. Of course, there seldom is with patients who aren't responsive when I first enter the room. I call the nurse and they listen to her heart. She has passed.

Signs of death

You'd think that after their training, doulas would be able to confirm if someone has died. But the truth is, if I call a patient's name or even poke the person and get no response, that doesn't mean the patient is dead. Sometimes it's not clear. One doula mentioned a patient who'd stopped breathing and the doula began counting and got up to 70. She believed the person had died, but then the patient took a deep breath, which was somewhat disconcerting since the doula assumed she had passed.

Pronouncing death can be tricky.

Today, when someone dies in a medical facility, the nurses generally listen to the patient's heart and take a pulse to make a determination. Medical personnel may hook the patient up to equipment that reads brain waves, respiration, and heartbeat. When the result is a flat line—and stays that way—it's probably a death. But even doctors make mistakes and may pronounce someone dead who is still alive. I've heard stories of patients waking up in morgues, still alive after their death has been called.

Death is treated in hospice and medicalized settings by specific scientific and medical observations. There's a protocol and when that protocol is satisfied, death is pronounced. While some of us may believe in something more beyond the physical, in hospice or medical institutions, death of the physical body is the final word.

As the nurses come in and the body is taken out, I leave to

go to another room. But first, I stop in the chapel to have a few moments to sit and hold sacred space and bid the patient to go with grace and ease.

Sacred Reflections

As I continue my work as a doula, I encounter not only spiritual and emotional lessons, but physical lessons about death and dying. It sounds hard to believe, but it's sometimes difficult to tell if someone has passed. At end of life, patients can be still, utterly quiet, and stop breathing. Yet, they are still alive. Sometimes, even if they're breathing, it's difficult to tell, because each inhale and exhale is so light it produces no obvious physical signs. So detecting death becomes a matter of medical confirmation that involves listening to the heart, checking brain waves, and respiration, which is when medical staff steps in. Doulas don't pronounce death. That's the job of the medical staff. It's the most profound moment in the care of a patient at end of life.

Lesson Seventeen: Each Passing is Different

It's only 4 am and I still have two hours to sleep before I have to get up. Since I'm not getting any younger, I need my rest. I try deep breathing and thinking about boring things, all to no avail.

I'm still thinking about Betty and all the patients I've sat with who've passed at hospice. At this point, there's been about twenty of them. The service I perform as a doula is ephemeral, but at the same time, very real. It may not seem as if I'm doing much, sitting beside the patient, but I'm in touch with their souls and that is a heavy matter. I feel them when I'm sitting there and feel them as they pass. And I wonder, will I feel them from the other side? Will they try to connect with me? I don't know. I've often "seen" the souls of those who've passed with emergency room or hospice nurses when I've read for them. These are patients who were grateful for the loving care and compassion that was provided for them at end of life by these caring souls.

I go round and round considering this until, finally, I roll out of bed at six and make myself a pot of tea. There's a get-together at work today and a class, so besides the regular duties, it'll be a busy day.

The role of security at hospice

As I enter the building, I notice a family sitting on the bench by the front entrance. I smile at them and they smile back. We all experience camaraderie here, as if we're family. In a way we are, because we're all connected to something greater.

When I check in, I say hello to the security guard. He's wearing his official-looking uniform with lots of badges. When I first started my work here I wondered why they'd need a security guard at hospice. I decide to ask him.

The security guard tells me about people trying to sneak into the rooms of hospice patients even when the family has prohibited visitors. It's his job is to tell them they can't go in. He also confides that quite a number of visitors show up inebriated. Some try to hide it, but others try to drink in the patients' rooms. Here, again, the guard must ask them to leave.

Family issues are huge in this setting, and things can occasionally get hostile. I've seen individuals erupt in acrimony over a parent or spouse. Families order a sibling or some other relative to leave. You would think that by the time a loved is in hospice, family and the dying have reached some kind of resolution with each other. That's not always the case.

It's clear the ill will is not about the patient at all —it's about conflicts between the relatives. In fact, much of our early hospice training included watching movies of acrimonious relatives at the bedside of ill family members. Unfortunately, this situation happens more frequently than anyone would like.

Some visitors become aggressive; others are angry about a loved one passing or because they are dealing with a crisis. Some people are angry because they thought they had things under control and now realize they don't.

The guard admits that as he tries to help everyone he's more of a therapist than a guard. He enjoys being a sounding board, though. It makes him feel like he's helping. Everyone I meet here wants to help. We all have that desire in common.

When someone is dying, balancing the needs of the visitors with the wishes of the person who is passing can be tricky.

I thank the guard for talking to me about his job. Everyone here does so much more than what their uniforms or official title indicate. When we work with illness and death, nothing falls within standard parameters.

I move towards the nursing station but hear laughter coming from the kitchen. The party for an aide who is retiring is underway. A buffet is spread out on the counter so before I begin my afternoon, I grab a tuna fish sandwich and wash it down with bottled water. I briefly think back to the high-flying parties of the investment business with firms renting out Lincoln Center, Bond girls circulating among the guests, or massage stations and live bands. Those days are over. The contrast with my current work at hospice couldn't be more different.

Today, I go from room to room to visit patients, who all have family members with them. It's lunchtime, sometimes the easiest time for family and friends to visit. They also tend to come more often as their loved ones get "closer."

A chat with a daughter

I check my watch. It's 12:30. I think about the woman with the flip-flops who was visiting the patient several days ago and decide to check to see if that patient is still here. I cross the hall and look inside and see the flip-flop woman is sitting with her loved one.

"Hi, I'm Debra," I say. "I'm a volunteer. Can I get you anything?"

"Oh, I saw you across the hall the other day and thought you were a family member," she says, extending her hand. "My name is Debra too." She moves to one side of the room gesturing for me to walk ahead towards the patient, her mother.

I move to her mother's bedside and listen to her heavy breathing. The daughter seems pained as her mother struggles for breath. I silently send a wish for the patient to be comfortable and at ease. Her breathing becomes more regular.

Debra tells me she doesn't know what to do with herself and is grateful for my company.

When I first started out at hospice, I thought this work would be difficult to do, since we work with the dying and their families and loved ones in intense circumstances. But I found that because I'm already in a helping profession, the work comes naturally. I ease right in and it's instinctual.

She tells me she has a sister who "only blows in once a year," and explains that she and her husband have assumed care for her mother over the years. Debra moves on to reminisce about her father, who died two years ago. She shares anecdotes about family members who sat in vigil at bedside only to have their loved one pass when they left to get a cup of coffee. She remarks that this seems to happen only with the older generation, but I'm not sure about that. It seems as if they go when the space and the time seem right.

We chat for an hour and she tells me more about her family. As we talk, I notice her mother's breathing seems to become more labored. Debra says the nurse recently gave her other pain medicine, but I offer to tell the nursing staff and see if they can do something more.

When I return from the nursing station I get ready to leave for the day, but stop when my cell phone vibrates. A text comes in asking if I can be a doula this evening for a 93-year-old woman at a long-term care facility. She probably won't make it through the night.

Yes. This is what I do.

As I leave Debra, she begins to sob. I feel her weight press against me as she hugs me and offers me an invitation. "Now there are more people to invite to Christmas dinner."

Sacred Reflections

Some patients pass in privacy, when you leave the room. Others are fine leaving surrounded by their loved ones. Each passing is different.

People choose when to leave in hospice in the process of dying. We all hear stories about someone slipping away as soon as you leave the room, which appears to be more than a random, coincidental observation. People seem in control of their dying, even in those last minutes when they appear to have nothing left.

Some people may delay dying until a significant date, such as a birthday, an anniversary, or something commemorative. Others who are about to die hold out until a family member arrives at their bedside. On the other hand, some folks die just before a special date, or before a loved one can get to their bedside, and seem unable to "let go" while family is present. They pass as soon as you leave the room, or before you arrive.

Dying is a private experience. Whether family is present or not, the separation into the other realm also means a kind of detachment from those who are here. And for the survivors, there's often a sense of feeling "left behind." You may have heard of family members or loved ones who say they are "angry" at the person who died, perhaps because of that feeling of being left behind.

And how it happens is determined by the person who is dying, whether they prefer to have their family surround them or a desire for a private and personal moment.

This also seems to suggest that our mind has some control over our last moments, of opting out of this reality. What makes this view controversial is that it's contrary to the way science views dying. Modern science sees our body as a machine. When the machine stops, it's over and that's when death occurs. But the concept that the moment of death may be determined by the mind is another perspective, suggesting yet again that much more is going on than we perceive.

Lesson Eighteen: We Feel Loved, Peaceful, and Safe as We Journey to Higher Realms

Today as I dress for work, I think about how good it feels to be part of this organization that helps so many. I feel honored to play even a small part here. Later, when I enter the facility, a volunteer at the front desk says, "Haven't seen you before. Do you usually work afternoons?"

I explain I'm usually there Monday and Thursday mornings but this week I'm doing the afternoon shifts.

When I scan the list of patients, I see only three marked for doulas. I ask the nurses and social workers if any of their patients are close.

"Room five," a nurse says. "The patient's family won't let him have any medication. He could use someone to sit with him."

This patient has COPD (chronic obstructive pulmonary disease). When the family could no longer care for him at home, they brought him to hospice. The staff wonders why he was brought here if he can't be medicated.

"He could benefit from someone holding his hand. He'd be a good one for you to sit with." The nurse pauses and looks at me expectantly as she waits to see if I have questions.

"Is he responsive?" I ask.

"No," she answers, "but he was yesterday."

The nurses seem upset that they can't administer medication, but there isn't much they can do. Hospice is about allowing a natural death to occur with dignity and without suffering, and sometimes staff is concerned this can only be maintained with medication.

While many families and patients think the benefits of hospice include protocols for pain and discomfort that can accompany death, others may fear these same protocols can hasten death. Or they may object to medications based on religious or ethical beliefs. In this case, it's unclear what the family is thinking.

In some cases, families and patients refuse medication, and vigils with candles and music are held at the patient's bedside in place of conventional treatment. But today, this is not the case and the staff is troubled.

I make my way down the hall, find room five and knock on the door. "Mr. Harris? My name is Debra. I'm a volunteer. Can I sit with you? Be comfortable," I say, as I enter the room.

The patient, who doesn't appear uncomfortable, is breathing thinly, as if climbing a mountain at a high altitude. His greying hair is fastened with elastic twists at the top of his head, and the light blue hospital gown fabric is covered with moons and stars.

"I'm going to stay with you," I say as I pull up a chair. I hold his frail, frail hand, soft and cool to the touch, as two nurses enter the room and take a breathing mask from his nightstand. They adjust it on his face and make sure it's on tight. If Mr. Harris tries to take it off, they say, I'm to use the red button next to the bed to call them.

With oxygen being administered, the patient seems comfortable and the nurses leave. I watch the muscles on his neck and chest move in and out. His hands rest on his abdomen as the mask seems to help him take deep breaths. His face has a pinkish tinge, which the nurses would describe by saying his color is good. I can't do much for Mr. Harris, but I can try to open a space that might be comfortable.

I concentrate on creating a relaxing sense of calm in the room and envelop it in a quiet energy. I watch Mr. Harris and feel the overhead fan sending cool air into the room as I breathe in and out. Cool air circulating in the room sometimes helps patients with respiratory issues. "Rest. You're doing fine," I murmur.

Ten minutes pass and a heavyset woman enters the room. She wears a name tag and an official-looking badge with her picture on it. She has a nice face—open and friendly. "You're sitting with Mr. Harris today?" she asks.

"Yes, I'm a doula," I say.

She identifies herself as the chaplain, and says, "Just holler if you need anything."

I tell her he's resting comfortably.

The chaplain nods and says, "That's good."

I don't often see chaplains in patients' rooms, but the staff is especially concerned about this patient and he's getting lots of attention. The fact that medication was refused concerns them.

No other visitors are present, so I continue to sit quietly with Mr. Harris. I turn the lights down and adjust the blinds so the room is dim.

I see Mr. Harris traveling to a restful spot, quiet and peaceful. His situation appears to be different from what had been mentioned about his condition earlier at the nursing station. Even without medication, he's traveling on a peaceful journey, where he feels at ease and safe. I feel a jolt of relief.

In a few minutes I look up and a tall, thin man in a yellow polo shirt and tan slacks enters the room. First he looks at the room number, as if he's checking to make sure he's in the right place. He then explains he grew up with Mr. Harris and is still a friend. "He's had so many health issues," a look of concern passes over his face. "This is my first time at hospice," he says. "Can I talk to him? Do I sit? I don't know what to do."

"Yes, you can talk to him. He hears you," I say. I gesture to the chair next to Mr. Harris. "Why don't you sit here?"

"I may just sit and read a little scripture." He puts his hand on Mr. Harris' shoulder. When he says, "Hi, George," the patient's eyelids flutter.

I stand and gather my belongings. "I'll let you have some privacy," I say.

He thanks me for being with his friend and I go on my way.

Sacred Reflections

Despite the lack of medication, Mr. Harris is on a journey to a peaceful place, much like others I've sat with. While one case doesn't make a trend, medication seems not to play a role in this particular patient's comfort. His journey of peace seems to be a part of his transition, notwithstanding the use of any psychoactive medication.

Sometimes cutting back on medication at end of life is the right thing to do, although it's a tough pill to swallow for many doctors and nurses, and sometimes for families and even patients, too. Discontinuing medications does not necessarily mean that symptoms will worsen, though. In this case, Mr. Harris seems to be in a state similar to other patients who had been administered a full panel of medications.

While hospice is supposed to provide comfort for the dying, our systems and body shut down naturally in the process of death. They know what to do. However, even while our systems seem programmed to follow this protocol, pain can still be an issue at end of life. But in the case of this patient, the process seems to be progressing smoothly.

In my work, I've seen patients routinely given medication and it's hard to know if all of it is necessary. Usually I see patients in a comfortable place and out of body anyway. However, I'm not a doctor or medical professional, and the medication issue is something each patient and family needs to come to terms with based on what feels right to them. Emotional issues may be at play too, just as strongly as the realities of administering medications and basic standards of care. At the end of the day, it's a tough call to make and, for anyone, a great responsibility.

Lesson Nineteen: We May Mention an "Appointment" to Keep at End of Life

At the start of my 11th month at work, after a morning walk and my gluten-free breakfast, I drive to work listening to NPR and then the classical music station. By the time I reach the turnoff thirty minutes later, I feel mellow and in the zone, ready for the day.

Today, I'm surprised when I enter the facility and see lots of people. I take in the families clustered in the hallways and a group chatting in the middle of the lobby. It's a weekend and families arrive on weekends to visit since work keeps so many away during the week. I realize that everyone who can make it, comes on the weekend.

I make my way around a group gathered next to a woman holding a baby and head straight to the nurses' station where two nurses are talking and a third is on the phone. Only twenty beds in the facility are filled today, and just one or two patients need a doula. The nurses mention the patient in room eight, a woman born in 1951, and the patient in room twenty-three, a man born in 1942. I visit eight first, but family is there and they say they're fine.

I weave down the hallway, past the visitors and carts, to room twenty-three. I knock, but there's no response. The room is dark as I enter and the patient, Mr. Walsh, is lying on his back, one eye open, snoring lightly. I take a breath as I assess the situation. A woman is sitting in a chair next to him.

I introduce myself and ask if I can get her anything.

"A glass of water," she says.

I return a few minutes later with a cup filled with water, which she drinks down in one gulp.

She wipes the back of her hand across her mouth and says, "Everyone here is so wonderful."

I agree, and then tell her to let me know if she needs anything.

Speaking in a hopeful tone, she says, "He's not going anywhere."

I nod and hope she's right for her sake. She seems optimistic and I sense she's not ready for him to leave yet. I hope she's able to spend more time with her loved one.

I stop by a few more rooms, and since everyone is fine, resting comfortably, I decide to visit Katherine, a patient I'd seen last week. I'm not sure what her diagnosis is, and she's not a hospice patient, but she's awake when I knock and enter.

She asks me if I'm "ready to go?" "I've been 'waiting' for you," she says, her eyes watching me.

I'm startled, but nod and think she must be getting close.

Hospice patients often speak in metaphors of their journeys. Sometimes they haven't said a word in days and then they ask about their train ticket or wonder where their hiking boots are. One woman said she wanted to go shopping on Friday and on Friday she died. This is not delusional talk. They are announcing their departures.

I turn back to Katherine and ask how she feels.

"It's my back. I have a lot of pain," she says.

I tell her I'll get her nurse so she can get some pain medication. I leave the room and let the nurse know about Katherine's pain. She in turn says she'll pass on the information to the patient's nurse.

One of the difficult things about working at hospice is feeling powerless over the many things I can't control. I can't ease Katherine's pain with medication, and can only report the issue to someone who can. That's the best I can do in a process that's greater than I am. Hospice has its own protocols and chain of authority, which is as it should be, of course, but it can still be frustrating.

Waiting for the bus

When I return to Katherine's room she turns her head slightly and mumbles, "I'm waiting for the man to come."

I straighten out her sheets and cover her bare legs.

Suddenly, she sits up. "There! It's him!" She points to the corner of the room.

I don't see him. But that doesn't mean I don't believe her, because we don't all see the same visions. However, I do see buses whizzing by, one after another in the other corner, but none are stopping for Katherine.

No one attempts to quantify or measure these encounters, sometimes referred to as "deathbed visions." I don't have all the answers about what they mean but I know in my heart they are true and real encounters.

Katherine isn't "journeying," but she seems to be in a stage marked by appointments and transportation related to a journey, which appear to be part of the process of the overall enfoldment. Patients first confirm they're going somewhere, and then they reference the type of transportation and appointments. Then they start their journey.

A moment later a doctor appears at the door and introduces himself. "Hi, I'm Dr. Veejay," he says, "I thought you were the patient's daughter."

Staff members often think the doulas are family visitors, but they soon recognize us as volunteers.

"How are you, dear?" he asks the patient.

The woman mumbles, "OK."

"You had a stroke," Dr. Veejay says.

"Stroke," the patient says. "God. He knows what happened."

"How's your vision? Can you see my finger?" the doctor asks as he holds up one, two, then three fingers.

"Stroke?" Katherine asks.

The doctor examines Katherine and says to press the nurse's button if she needs anything.

As the doctor leaves, a nurse enters the room.

"I'm just giving you your medication," the nurse says to Katherine.

The patient mumbles.

"What did you say?" The nurse leans over the bed and shakes her head. As she heads to the door to leave, she thanks me for being there.

"I don't know exactly what I can do for this patient," I say.

"All you have to do is provide a therapeutic presence." With that, the nurse leaves and I consider how my interactions with non-doula patients are so different from doula patients, who are generally non-responsive. Even if a non-doula patient doesn't do much except mumble and attempt to converse, there's still another level of connection that takes place between us as I do my best to assist them. In this case, at least Katherine recognizes and interacts with me.

I look at the thin blanket covering Katherine's legs and ask if she's cold and needs a blanket.

She says yes, so I cross the hall, passing by other rooms on my way to the supply closet, stacked with towels, sheets, and blankets. I pull out a white blanket and hurry back to Katherine's room where I stretch the blanket out over her legs.

She points to the corner and mumbles again. I lean closer to try to understand but at first I can't make out the words.

Then she points to the corner where I saw the buses whizzing past. I hear her say, "I'm waiting for the bus."

I see she's waiting patiently for her turn. She's not at all agitated.

Patients seem to know it is their assignment to wait; that is all they have to do. Just wait. I glance at my watch. There are still a few minutes until I have to leave, so I relax as Katherine moves comfortably along on her journey while I sit silently beside her.

Sacred Reflections

Patients at end of life may reference appointments or meetings, or transportation to catch. They may say they are going home. These are metaphors for the journey they're about to take. There are many anecdotal accounts of patients referencing days, dates, and even times of "meetings," which coincide with time of death. It's just another aspect of the realities that open up at end of life.

When terminal patients talk about catching buses or trains or other transportation, it's often their way of predicting when they're going to die. One Sunday evening, a high-powered executive checked herself into hospice and said she had a meeting on Monday morning, and that's when she died.

A young man who had been in and out of hospice was a baseball fan and talked often about "opening day." At one point, he checked himself into hospice and decided he didn't want to be maintained anymore. It was opening day and the man's nurse and his wife put the game on. The first pitch was thrown out, and the patient died.

These are not isolated examples. They demonstrate that our mind is connected to a larger, eternal reality. It's a fascinating observation and begs the question, how does the mind know how to coordinate with the universe? Regardless, it also demonstrates that death is more than the decline of the physical body, and that the mind and universal consciousness play a larger role.

Lesson Twenty: Personal Items Add Energy and Love to a Patient's Room

Last night I fell into an uneasy sleep, dreaming of journeys, tickets, and appointments. I finally roll out of bed at 5:00 am, make a cup of tea, and grab my laptop to check my messages before I shower and head to hospice for the day. As I make my way up the driveway, a family of baby geese passes in front of my car. I wait for them to cross before going the rest of the way to the lower parking lot.

It's a warm, sunny spring day. The lemony fragrance of magnolia blossoms drifts from the garden and sweetens the air. The peaceful quiet is interrupted only by the sound of car doors slamming as groups of visitors arrive for the morning.

The front door is open so I walk in and go directly to the nurses' station.

"No need for doulas today," I say to the group of nurses. "It's quiet."

"Don't say that!" one says. "That means we're going to get slammed. Whenever it's quiet, there's a rebound."

Another nurse suggests I go to rooms twenty-four and twenty-eight. Both have elderly patients—one is 100 years old, the other, 95. Neither is actively dying, but they're both by themselves and unresponsive.

I knock first on twenty-four and a man asks me to come in, so the patient isn't alone after all. A youthful-looking man sits beside the woman, who is sitting up in bed. She is the 100-year-old patient. I introduce myself and ask if I can get them anything.

"You need anything, Mom?" the son asks.

The woman mumbles something I don't understand.

"Thank you," he says. "I think we're good here."

I nod and say if there is anything they need, to let us know.

As I leave the room, I check the roster again. The 95-year-old woman is in the next room. I get no response when I knock on her door. I enter the room, and although it's a bright, sunny day, the blinds are drawn and the room is dark.

"I'm a volunteer, Mrs. Perez. Are you doing okay?"

The woman is lying on her back with a tube in her nose, breathing steadily, snoring lightly, her eyes flickering.

"I'll sit with you while you rest," I whisper, taking a seat in the leather chair next to her bed. "You be easy," I say, also breathing quietly, comfortable with the silence.

Admitted two days ago, the patient has a mass and a perforation, but she appears comfortable. I check her diet. It's clear liquids, which is different from the 100-year-old patient next door, whose dietary preference as noted on the roster is "Pleasure."

A pleasure diet indulges a patient's special requests. In these cases, a patient with diabetes can have candy, the person on a gluten-free diet gets regular wheat pasta. The food in a pleasure diet is meant for just that, pleasure and enjoyment, even if these patients have been on a strict special diet. Most of the patients on the roster today are on regular diets, since most are not actively dying and can probably feed themselves or eat with assistance.

I'm glad to see photos and personal objects in this patient's room. Too often, these rooms are empty—totally devoid of any personal objects or ties to the patients. Photographs and personal mementos are wonderful ways to raise the energy and personalize the space, no matter the length of stay. Photos in patient rooms should portray happiness so the energy they carry in these rooms is positive. Picture boards or a collection of photos are also nice ways to see how our loved ones' lives progressed, how they were with family and friends. They help create a complete picture of the patient as an individual. Personal objects can also uplift the energy in the room. Handmade items like artwork or a quilt are also wonderful for this.

The only sound in Mrs. Perez's room is the steady trickling

of water coming from a closet where a bottle of sterile water is plugged into an inhaler. As I look around the room, I shake my head. The patient's husband in Spirit is in the corner, by the window. His presence is strong and powerful.

"I love you," he tells his wife. *"You're coming back to me now. I'll take your hand and ease your way and together we'll cross."*

"Sometimes we need a hand to help us to the other side," he explains to me.

He begins speaking to his wife again. *"I'll go with you step by step, and we'll pick our way, stepping on the stepping stones. I'll be holding you, never letting you go. You'll feel my presence."*

These communications, which I witness regularly here at hospice, show me that our significant relationships continue on the other side. Not only do loved ones meet us at end of life to help us transition, others with whom we've had relationships continue too, not just those that are most significant to us. Mothers and daughters. Grandparents and children. Pets, too. Even those who had painful relationships, such as fathers who may have been abusive, or children who passed traumatically, are healed and may be with other loved ones in a higher dimension and meet us.

Patient after patient see their loved ones and communicate with them in Spirit. It is one of the most meaningful parts of the process and demonstrates the bridge between the earthly plane and higher dimensions, the continuity of the Soul, and the karmic aspects of relationships.

Those in Spirit may be sitting on the bed or standing on the side of the room. They may be near the ceiling or at the foot of the bed. It's remarkable that they all seem to be doing the same thing as if it is programmed in by some higher force.

While so many in our culture trust that science has—or will have—all the answers to most everything, science doesn't have an answer to the Spirit connection at end of life. (Unless their answer is simply to label the experiences as "hallucinations.")

But if you've ever had an extraordinary experience, this continuity in Spirit may make sense to you; or you may have had experiences that enable you to relate to what happens in hospice.

I watch as Mrs. Perez's shoulders and chest move up and down slightly. The door to the room opens, and a nurse in white scrubs peeks in.

I greet her, but she simply nods and backs out, slowly closing the door behind her. I guess she thinks I'm family.

Mrs. Perez's husband begins to communicate again.

"My wife thought she couldn't do this on her own. But she's carried on just fine. Now she's resting. She was a fighter and her faith kept her going."

I hear a stirring and the patient shifts slightly and sighs, perhaps in response to her husband's comments.

I ask Mr. Perez how he is.

"Everyone on earth thinks dying is something special. Something that needs to be kept a secret. Something that's too difficult to talk about. But there's really nothing to it. The truth is, we're here all along. We're this close." He shows me his palms pressed together. *"Very little separates us, just the pictures painted by those who don't understand.*

But we are love. Ever present. You slide in and don't even notice it. And when you're here, you realize it's the most comforting place you've ever been. It's the height of fulfillment, the height of perfect light and space.

Death is something dreamed up by people on earth. Here we think in terms of perfection. Death refers only to your physical body and applies to earth, but has no relevance anywhere else in the universe or in the realms we can move between."

I take in what the husband has to say and listen, just as I listen to those who've passed over when I'm engaged in a reading. The husband, like all those on the other side, is real and permanent and his comments and conversation seem completely natural to me. I always listen to those who've crossed over and pay attention, because many of them have a wisdom we on earth lack. Of course, others might not feel that way. But as a medium, I am used to this type of conversation with those on the other side.

"How do you experience love?" I ask.

"Love is all there is. It's in the air we breathe in these parts. It defines our existence. It's the fabric woven into our air, the chain of life in heaven. It ties us together and there's never any slippage."

A doctor I've seen before knocks and enters the room. We say hello and he raises the bed and leans over. Mr. Perez stands aside watching.

"Are you able to squeeze my fingers?" the doctor asks. "Can you wiggle your toes for me?" He checks under the blanket and feels to see if she is wiggling her toes, and uses the flashlight on his phone to look at her face. "All right, my dear, can I get you anything?" he asks. "Can I get you anything?" he asks again louder. "Can you hear me?"

"I'm fine," she responds.

The doctor glances at me and remarks that she needs her hearing aid.

"Why does she have a tube in her nose?" I ask.

"Oxygen," he says. "Everyone gets oxygen now whether you need it or not. It used to be Foley catheters, now it's oxygen." I take this remark as his way of letting me know his view of today's health care regulations.

We say goodbye and he moves on to the next room. Patient time is measured here in minutes, so there's little time to see fully what's taking place.

I check on the patient again. She is walking down a road, moving forward, saying, "I can do this. Nothing will get in my way."

Her husband stands to the side and watches her move forward.

I adjust her pillows and check my watch. 11:00 am. Time to

move on to the next patient.

"Goodbye, Mrs. Perez," I say. "You take care and I'll be seeing you."

She shifts and nods at me. I thank her husband, and he sends a band of beautiful healing white light.

Sacred Reflections

I think about Mrs. Perez surrounded by her memories and objects that retain her energy and relate to her personal story, even if she doesn't see or appear cognizant of them. Energy isn't static. It's alive, and objects significant to us retain our energy. In addition to the meaning they hold for us, these special items may be invested with divine vibrations.

No one should think of a dying person as an empty suit. The dying are still here. Treat them with love. In general, it's important to create balance and harmony in our living and working spaces—our environment—but it's especially applicable to the rooms of the dying.

While I am all in favor of spiffing up and personalizing a room's decor, I don't recommend essential oils, smudging, or other similar practices that change the sounds and smells in a patient's room at end of life. Patients don't need this, and it's the wrong thing for their bodies at this time. Their astral bodies are already getting what they need. The dying are sensitive and this is not the time to incorporate new energies.

That said, rituals can personalize events when we, family and friends, grasp at straws for anything to soothe us and feel better in the midst of our impending loss. Creating memory quilts or collages or scrapbooks serve multiple purposes: They're reminders that people care and provide a living energy and a context that helps all who come into the room develop a greater understanding of the patient. These items are left behind for family and friends to revisit later too. Any kind of ritual or ceremony can personalize and create meaning at a time when meaning is so desperately sought.

There are many opportunities at hospice to create powerful rituals around death and enhance a loved one's room with personal objects. However, we don't see this enough. Rituals or personal mementos don't need to be elaborate or fancy, but even small efforts, like some photographs, can promote connection to the experience and help people come to terms—and come together. Perhaps by personalizing these spaces at end of life, we also can erase or adjust some of the stigma associated with death.

Lesson Twenty-One: Granting Permission to Die Is Implicit

The summer heat won't quit, and when I arrive at hospice the temperature hovers around 95 degrees. Sweat trickles down my back, and when thoughts of jumping into a pool fill my head, I decide to head to the community pool immediately after my shift and get in some laps.

Twelve months have passed since the first day I stepped into the room of a dying patient, and I've come a long way. Much that surrounds this mystery we call death is so little understood, and even less appreciated. That our essence can persist in different dimensions and carry on after death is still not a widely accepted idea across all religions and cultures. Who governs this process? I wonder. Why is there consistency across experiences and what is the meaning of it all? And what does it mean for the bigger picture?

Taking our time

Today, as I head to the first room, I focus on being present. I smile and knock lightly on the door of the first patient, a 58-year-old woman who has been in hospice for a month. I introduce myself as she continues to breathe, but is otherwise motionless in bed. The bedcovers are pulled up to her shoulders. At the top of her bed, four Mylar balloons say, "Happy Birthday!"

As I take a seat, a nurse enters the room.

"Mrs. Clyde, it's Rachel the nurse. I'm going to give you your meds." She injects her with a syringe. "I talked to Steven and Sarah this morning. They're all checking on you. Steven says he can't come in today. They all say it's okay for you to go, whenever you're ready."

The nurse turns to me. "She hasn't eaten in a month. She's been like this, unresponsive, for a week. The family keeps telling her it's okay to go. We can't figure out why she's still here."

I ask if she often tells the patients it's okay to leave. I don't want the patient to hear me, so I whisper my question.

"The family's been telling her to leave," she says, defensively. "I don't usually say that, but they've been talking that way. Her birthday was yesterday. We thought she'd leave after that but something is keeping her here. We can't figure it out." Pinching her thumb and index finger together, she adds, "Medicine really only understands this much."

She talks about the medication the patients receive and remarks that a lot is driven by the patients' families. When patients become agitated, the families ask for more medication. But this nurse says she believes the families need to offer more support, so the medical staff can cut back on the medication patients are given.

A doctor enters the room. "It's Dr. Janet, just checking on you, Mrs. Clyde." She shakes her head at the nurse as if to wordlessly communicate, *"Can you believe she's still here?"* The doctor checks the patient's pulse. "Weak." She shakes her head again.

Dr. Janet and the nurse thank me and then leave to continue their rounds.

I check the roster. The patient just turned 58 yesterday. A tray of food and juices sit untouched on her dresser and nightstand.

As I create space in the room, I see the patient is traveling to a higher dimension. She is so comfortable she doesn't want to leave that higher realm and has attached herself to it. Telepathically, I ask why she hasn't left and if she's okay.

"Well, I like what comes with being alive. I have my family, my friends, my faith. I'm engaged with my life. There is no one thing keeping me here, the way the doctors think. It's just that I'm defined by my connections."

"Are you comfortable?" I ask.

"It's okay," she says, *"it takes some getting used to."* She gasps a bit and catches her breath.

"And are you getting used to it?" I ask.

"I don't want to rush things."

I can see that she's taking her time.

"I have some pain but I don't mind… it's way down there," she says, indicating a much lower vibration than where she is now.

"Your family gave you permission to leave," I say. "Does that matter to you?"

"I'll make up my own mind. I'm doing this myself. Don't get me wrong. I love my family, but folks seem to think that if they tell you it's okay to leave, that you're going to go. But I have my own reasons. I have my own destiny and I'm turning on this car when I'm ready. I'll do it when the time is right."

It's funny that she uses the metaphor of the car. It turns out, when she passes a few days later and I read her obituary, that she worked in an auto body shop.

"When will you know if the time is right?" I ask.

"When God tells me," she says.

"Is faith important to you?" I ask.

"Very," she says. *"I believe, but that's not the whole picture I'm getting here."*

I see what's transpiring, the immensity of what's occurring, beyond any earthly dimensions.

She says she's talking with a few others who are trying to tell her it's okay. *"This is like a family meeting, where you're briefed about something coming up."*

At least one of the people talking to her is her grandfather, who's saying Mrs. Clyde can come and be with him. But Mrs. Clyde is her own person, and she's still making decisions her own way.

I watch the covers move up and down as Mrs. Clyde continues to breathe steadily. Besides the occasional sound of her breathing, there's no other sign of life in the room.

I look around the room and her mother in Spirit is also there.

"She was always so independent," she says. *"She always had to*

do things her way! Let me tell you, that woman kept me on my toes."

"Does she know you're here?" I ask the question, although I believe I already know the answer.

"Yes, she sure does," she says, *"and she's grateful, but she feels like Momma is always trying to get her to do things her way."*

Her response seems to echo what I've witnessed of the end-of-life process. Everyone does it their own way.

"My sister is here too," she says. *"We're together all the time."*

"What do you do on the Other Side?" I ask. "How do you spend your time?"

"Well, I like being with my family. I always enjoyed them, so here I'm with my sister a lot. Sometimes all of us in my family get together, like we used to, only here we just enjoy each other's company and our energies meld and grow as we get together. Sometimes those on earth can feel it."

Of course, not everyone is going to be good with the idea of spending eternity with their families. What we do in the afterlife is very much an individual decision, so no worries that everyone is stuck with their family for eternity.

"Why do you come in when a family member leaves?"

"This is our job. It's part of what we do here. We know when someone's leaving and we go to look after them and create a circle of guidance, in the true sense of guides. We have a job to do and it's an important job. It comes with our passing," she says.

"When someone passes, we join a circle of love. It's a bridge, so those who are passing see and know we're still here, that we still live. That we didn't go anywhere, and we're the same as we ever were. It helps them cross, when it's their time to leave.

It's our assignment. Like you might show up for an assignment at work if you knew it was your time to do a duty," she says. *"We stand aside when we appear but at the same time, they know we're there. We go every time we're called."*

It's comforting, isn't it, the idea that family in Spirit come in when loved ones are passing, so they won't be alone, on their own?

The communication between those at end of life and those on the other side is the equivalent of tying sheets together when we evacuate a building. There's a chain that allows the dying to transition. It is part of the process, although we can't say why. I can't explain it, but it appears to be what occurs.

End of life visitations have been referenced through the ages, but skepticism still surrounds them. Particularly in health care. They're rarely talked about, and considered hallucinations to be "treated" with Haldol. But what I witnessed never seemed like hallucinations to me. These visions seem to be a part of the end of life and patients accept them peacefully. No one shrieks in fear or yells at them to go away.

"Who calls you?" I ask.

"It's just something we know to do. We have duties over here, you know. Big duties. We accept them and no one ever says no. 'No' isn't something that comes up here. Once you graduate to come here, you know you are at another level of existence and service that comes with higher responsibilities. We all feel it's a blessing to be called—that's one of our main duties."

Throughout my communication with Mrs. Clyde's loved ones, she continues to rest comfortably, unmoving in bed.

"My body's not ready to go yet," she says. *"I could stay here for a hundred years."*

So, even though her body is nearly gone—I bet she doesn't weigh more than ninety pounds—she's not ready.

"Be comfortable," I say, checking the clock and seeing it's 2:30. I've been in Mrs. Clyde's room for one and a half hours. It seems much shorter since I've met and conversed with her family in Spirit for some of that time.

"Take care, Mrs. Clyde." I rest my hand on her shoulder through the covers. She is barely holding on. "Be comfortable and at ease."

Later, when I sign out and indicate in the notes that I sat with her, I see her diagnosis is liver cancer. She's a fighter, though. A few days later, I learn she passed.

Sacred Reflections

According to conventional wisdom, it's a positive, loving act to give our loved ones "permission" to leave. But I question that now and believe the concept needs to be reconsidered.

Some tell the dying they'll be okay without them or let them know they don't need to stay. Some others even encourage them by saying it's okay to "cross over." According to Pallimed, a blog on hospice and palliative medicine, when patients are actively dying they may become fearful, which is why some people hang on for what our earthbound selves call, "so long." However, dying is a process and according to this blog, "... sometimes permission to stay until they're ready to go is really what's needed."

I sit at the bedside of many dying patients where nurses urge the family to tell the patient to pass. And family members, having heard this is the right thing to do, tend to go along. Some families, one by one, give a dying loved one permission to go. I've heard stories about families encouraging this passing many times. But the patients just aren't ready.

Telling our loved ones that it's okay to leave may merely be our response to a belief that we can manage death, that *we* can control the situation. But from what I see, the universe and the dying have it under control. It seems our bodies and minds know what to do. We know when the time is right, and we progress in accordance with our own plan.

Still, since this idea of granting permission has taken hold I hear many stories about telling someone it was okay to pass, and sure enough, the person died. But did these individuals really pass because they were told it was okay, or did they pass because they made a choice based on their own destiny?

Since this is a process, after all, which unfolds differently for each of us, we only need to stand aside and let our loved ones proceed. We can let this happen with grace and with an all-knowing intelligence guiding the experience.

Lesson Twenty-Two: Angels and Celestial Caregivers Assist Us at End of Life

Today it's so busy I can't find a parking space. I circle the lot and end up leaving my car farther down the hill. When I hike up the path, I see cars from Maryland, Pennsylvania, Massachusetts, Florida, Maine. Families have come from far away to visit their loved ones today.

The front desk is unmanned so I make my way to the nursing station where I hear some nurses chatting about their patients. One in particular is concerned about medicating a patient. "I keep giving him medication but it's not making a difference," she says. "He's not more comfortable. It's just making him more out of it."

As I sign in, one of the nurses says his 92-year-old patient, Sidney, could use some company. The patient's son is coming back later, but for now he's alone and company would be good.

I knock on the patient's door and find a heavyset man lying on his back with a breathing tube in place. Sidney is resting comfortably under two layers of white hospital blankets. His tray table is littered with potato chips, pancake syrup, hard candies, ginger ale, Styrofoam containers, and plastic utensils. He has been a patient in hospice for 52 days.

I put my cell phone on silent and turn down the volume of the Fox News Channel on the TV. I adjust Sidney's covers and touch his shoulder. His energy seems fine, even, and constant.

As I pull up a chair, I see he's reliving the early years of his life, watching the scene from above his body. He seems pleased by the progress he's made and this creates peace of mind for him.

"I have come so far," he says. *"I always believed I could achieve something better and I lived the kind of life others only dream about. Those early years gave me a strong foundation. It's all about thinking*

you can do it. Don't ever let anything stop you. When I had setbacks, I realized they could only stop me momentarily. My life was determined by whatever I wanted to achieve and I always kept that in mind."

Sidney believed in the power of positivity and it sounds like he was a pretty good manifester, too. That is, he could make his goals and dreams a reality.

"This is an interesting journey," he says, appearing to respond when I wonder if he's comfortable. *"It's a wonderful time to review everything I've experienced. I'm able to watch it again but from a different perspective."*

Like other patients, Sidney is reviewing his life and appears grateful to have experienced these rich moments. Yet, he also seems to accept that they were a part of his life's journey and that he will move on from here. Sidney's case is not unique at end of life.

The good news is that we really do reach a stage of letting go as we prepare to pass. The universe has a way of taking care of this when we approach end of life. There's a "line" you cross as you near the exit at which point you let go. You don't consider those earthly issues any more. They're not in the forefront of your consciousness. They disappear. They are low vibration energies and have no place in the afterlife. They're part of the package of living on earth, not meant to be taken with us.

Part of this is accomplished at end of life because what we see in our journey of passing is so divine and beautiful that it becomes all that matters. Not only does the material world not concern us, but the issues left undone shrink in importance as we experience a shift. The force of the metaphysical world takes over and we are content with the shift. It is true and beautiful and has meaning.

Ever since I first began this work, I sensed there was a reason I chose it. When I consider what these patients are telling me, I realize there are always so many lessons to learn.

A nurse knocks on the door and enters the room. "Mr.

Santorum? I have your medicine. Do you think you can wake up to take your medicine?" she asks as she touches him. He murmurs but doesn't wake up.

"I'll have to come back later when he's awake," she says.

She and I clear his food trays, throwing away the empty cups, the leftover food, the trash left by visitors. Not only does it tidy up the room, but it helps to clear the energy too.

"He hasn't been eating," she says. "Patients lose their interest in food, sleep more and are less responsive as they get closer, although he seems at ease."

I agree. He does seem to be in harmony with the process.

She gets ready to leave and thanks me for sitting with the patient.

Within minutes, a volunteer enters the room. "I'm Clara, a volunteer," she says. "Are you a doula?"

Everyone's interested in us doulas. I tell her I am.

"Well, my job is stocking the refrigerators," she says. "And I stop and see the patients on Tuesdays. I don't really spend much time with them though. I don't know if I could do what you do." She looks at Sidney lying unresponsive in bed.

I've found that even other hospice volunteers view doulas as peculiar—different—animals. Even here there's speculation that others who work at hospice couldn't do doula work.

Clara and I chat for a few minutes before she leaves. Then I watch the patient from my chair beside his bed. He appears to be at the edge of the stars, just beyond this world. He looks as if he could reach out and touch them.

His heart chakra is bursting with universal love. He's grateful for everyone who has touched his life. He is a very generous and loving man, and I sense he's lived a complete and full life.

"*I always believed there was something greater than myself,*" he says. "*And now I am connected with it and see its true power. This is more beautiful than any of my memories.*"

I glance around the room. Many men in Spirit are present

with him—his grandfather, a brother, and other male relatives are clustered on the side of the room.

All the men defer to Sidney's grandfather.

"My grandson is a wonderful man," the grandfather says. *"With a kind heart. He knows we are here and we'll take his hand when the time calls for it."*

As I gaze at the patient, I see angels hovering over his head. This is another aspect of my mediumship. I'm able to see those who have crossed over, but also guides, angels, and other entities. This is what comes of having the ability to see beyond our world. These angels are busy administering to Sidney and gently sending beams of love and golden light to him.

While mediumship may seem illusive and improbable to you, the truth is that if you've ever been "visited" by a deceased loved one in a dream, or entered a room and caught the hint of your late father's cigar smoke or the scent of your grandmother's favorite lavender perfume, these are also mediumistic experiences. The only difference between you and me is that I have additional training that enhances my abilities.

"We work hard with lightness and love," the angels say. Other angels hover over his body, celestial caregivers.

There are many types of angels but these particular ones seem to be working with the patient's soul in preparation for death. They are as wispy as air but with a grand energy as they pour their blessings on us.

Angels assist us in specific ways. Some attend to our aura. Others make sure we are comfortable. Some bring in a gentle energy that allows them to do their work. As a medium, I see angels and they are with all of us, and it is their pleasure to help in myriad ways. All we need to do is ask. Many people, I've found, don't realize that we have these higher realm "helpers" with us. But they are always there, just waiting to be called upon. These angels are working with the patient's body, bringing in a loving light.

In a few minutes there's a knock on the door and a handsome young man enters. I introduce myself and he says he's the patient's grandson, visiting from New York.

"Would you like to spend some time with your grandfather?" I ask.

He nods. "I'll be here for about two hours."

I tell him I'll leave them alone and stand to say goodbye. The grandson thanks me and I wish them well, and send them both blessings.

Sacred Reflections

History and mythology are full of references to angels that connect us with a powerful but gentle source energy, and many people say they have deathbed visions of angels or aspects of light at death. While I can't prove to you that angels exist, it seems we're accompanied by strong spiritual presences at end of life. I believe that not only do we not die alone, but we have extraordinary help in the most protective and benevolent way in life and at death.

From what I have seen, we appear to have a "spiritual team" made up of loved ones and divine participants who step up when we pass. As a medium, I frequently see guides as well as angels and ancestors who are with us to provide a protective and loving service. Their work is to serve and guide us to the greatest and highest good, and they work with us throughout life and at end of life. Our angels and guides serve in all sorts of capacities from the simple "parking angels" to the more profound "health and well-being" guides. They're part of a collaborative effort that is preordained, eternal, and sacred. Here on earth, the medical staff is busy tending to our physical body, but our etheric body is being tended by a higher source that completes the picture. The angels I watched did their work in an extraordinary but subtle way, with delicacy and a full helping of love and light. I was impressed by this work, so beautiful, so full, and such an important part of the overall transformation of our consciousness, yet done unobtrusively.

Like other aspects of the invisible realm, all we need to do is tune in and begin to pay attention, and soon we may be able to feel or sense these energies. Once we recognize them, our personal bond will solidify and we can begin to call on them for assistance.

Lesson Twenty-Three: Synchronicity Exists in Life and Death

When I arrive at hospice, I see there's been a special event earlier this morning, a get-together for an aide who is retiring. I know this because two aides are wheeling a cart of soft drinks and wicker baskets full of breakfast pastries past the front desk. When I get to the desk, a few volunteers are signing in as others are leaving. I check the roster and decide to start upstairs, where patients in rooms thirty-five and thirty-nine need a doula today.

I start with room thirty-five, but a sign on the closed door says no one is to enter. A nurse nearby says she thinks the patient and his wife are napping. Another nurse suggests I go to thirty-nine. The patient's wife is usually with him, but she's left for now.

Watching and waiting

"Thomas," I call, lightly tapping on his door. "I'm Debra. I'm a volunteer." I don't expect a response, and when I enter the room, Thomas is on his back, with the bedcovers pulled up to his neck. I see one hand curled up by his cheek. The rest of his body is covered by a light white blanket. His mouth is slightly open and he breathes deeply and comfortably.

The television is on to a soap opera, showing a scene of a patient in bed, dressed in a hospital gown, on a breathing machine. A visitor knocks on the door and enters the television patient's room.

I take a seat next to the patient, and within minutes, a man comes in and says he's Thomas' oldest friend. "We've been friends since the third grade."

He leans over Thomas and says, "Can you hear me? I want to tell you that I love you. And Mary loves you too. Very much." He holds his friend's hand and pulls the covers up a bit more. I notice the friend, like many other visitors, has a bit of nervous energy that's channeled into adjusting the bedcovers when they don't really need it, unconsciously keeping his hands busy. I've done this same thing myself.

He tells me Thomas' breathing has changed since his last visit several days ago. "It's much more labored," he says. He looks distressed and I reach out my hand. He holds it tightly for a moment then lets go. Then he says Thomas has been at hospice for ten days.

A few minutes pass in peaceful silence, interrupted when the doctor enters the room.

"Has Thomas been grimacing?" she asks. "Is he responsive?"

The doctor tells the patient she is going to listen to his heart, but Thomas doesn't respond. When she's done, the friend asks for additional information about Thomas, but the doctor can't provide it because of HIPAA, the Health Insurance Portability and Accountability Act, which protects personal medical records.

As the doctor leaves, the friend says, "He was the last person I expected this to happen to."

"Tell me about Thomas," I say.

"He was so kind," he says. "We used to jog together in the local park every day." He shakes his head sadly. "We met when we were eight years old and have been best friends ever since."

The friend goes on to tell me about Thomas' brain tumor and the surgery just weeks ago. He pushes Thomas' hair back to show me the scar on the patient's forehead. He says that his sister had the exact same kind of brain tumor two years earlier. "Isn't that odd?" he asks.

No, not so odd, I think. There's synchronicity everywhere.

"My sister died, but Thomas supported me through the whole ordeal."

"I'm so sorry," I say, nodding to show I understand how difficult this is for him.

"How much worse can this get?" the friend asks.

I shake my head. I don't have that kind of expertise and can't say.

Then he asks what people—family members, visitors, nurses, doctors, virtually everyone—always ask. *Why do you do this work?* I repeat my experience with hospice during my mother's illness and that, as a result, I felt a calling.

A few minutes later, another friend, a woman, knocks on the door. The two friends exchange a hug and the new friend pulls up a chair next to the bedside. I offer to leave them alone to give them privacy with the patient. They thank me as they sit on either side of the bed.

I leave and make my way to another room, passing unopened boxes of exam gloves, sterile wipes, and boxes of tissues stacked in the hall. I'm reminded that no matter how homey the facility is, you never really forget you're in a medical facility. I'm interrupted by a volunteer, who stops to chat and tells me a friend of hers is in a room down the hall—with a brain tumor.

I go from room to room to check on the patients but all of them have family members with them today. That doesn't surprise me because it's lunchtime, and for many family and friends it's the easiest time to visit.

No one needs a doula today. No restless patients, no one trying to smoke. No commotion in the halls. Few people dying, and those who are here are quiet.

I speak with one of the aides about the situation that day, and she says everything here is cyclical and no one knows why. "First, we'll get a lot of patients with pancreatic cancer. Then quite a few have lung cancer, and next, it seems many have brain tumors. Then it will be quiet for weeks with only a few people dying."

Today is one of those quiet days. Only a few patients and nice families.

"Being here isn't for everyone," the aide adds. "Some people can't handle it, so they don't visit. And death is seen differently here at hospice."

"What do you mean?" I ask.

"In the city, people are accustomed to getting a phone call from the police telling them someone was shot and died," the aide says. The contrast with hospice is obvious. "Many people aren't accustomed to even the idea of hospice."

I think about what the aide said about patterns in hospice; patterns in types of disease and patient census. The causes of the final illnesses seem to occur in bunches. I don't take it lightly. I believe patterns exist everywhere, including here.

I never thought of synchronicity in the realm of death and dying, but why not? If there's synchronicity in life, why not in death? The law of attraction exists across all realms, as we intersect with each other and the energies of the universe.

Sacred Reflections

There's a connection in our world of matter which affects all things and this connection shows up in our lives and also shows up in death. Patterns exist and if we stand back, we may see them. They may take the form of multiple patients with the same diagnosis, or a relative and friend dying of the same illness. Or people from the same town or school or community admitted at the same time as hospice patients.

We are all on interconnected journeys and our higher awareness intersects and organizes this with other broader realities. Is there a hidden meaning in this? What are we to make of it? Are we in fact just living in a holographic universe where reality and how we experience it is not real?

I'm done thinking this is a coincidence. I don't believe in coincidences. I pay close attention to synchronicities since there's usually a message there, a reason we are brought to these situations. Today, I heard stories about brain tumors, too many seemingly "random" stories to call them a coincidence. The universe is saying that we need to pay attention to its messages, even if we don't immediately understand or recognize their meaning. But if we sit with them for awhile, we may uncover the deeper meanings.

Lesson Twenty-Four: As We Ascend, We Pass Through Ever Higher Levels of Consciousness

We're in the thick of summer, with today's temperature nearing 100 degrees. Only my billowy dress and lightweight sandals give me any hope of staying cool. As I walk the fifty or so yards from my car to the building, beads of sweat trickle down my neck and back. A blast of cool air hits my face as I walk into the air-conditioned lobby. I see a crowd of nurses, aides, and volunteers celebrating an employee's birthday. There's a Carvel ice cream cake, balloons and streamers and a side table filled with gifts—a coffee mug, a travel tote, a sweater with the logo of the facility and packages covered in bright wrapping paper.

No patient rosters are at the nursing station, so an aide prints one up for me and I round the corner to the printer to retrieve one. As I wait for the paper, I check out the notices on the wall and see flyers for a picnic, a poster advertising a uniform sale, a notice about electronic death certificates, and a seminar on wound care management. Thank you cards and letters are taped to the wall and obituaries are stuck in between. This office references death and dying, and I can't help but compare it to my former office with its notices of squash and golf tournaments, sailing outings and cocktail parties at private clubs.

While all 41 beds are filled today, only three patients need a doula.

A nurse greets me in the hall and suggests I check upstairs and then see the patient in room seven.

I make my way up the two sets of stairs to the upper level, and once I reach it, a nurse at the nurses' station says the patient in room thirty-three needs me. I go through my usual routine of knocking on the patient's door lightly and making my presence known by calling out my name.

The patient's name is Mr. Samuels. He's on his back in bed, motionless, a breathing tube attached to his neck. He's had a tracheotomy and the buildup of fluids is being drained with an oxygen machine that whispers away in the corner. His mouth is slightly open, and like others at end stage, he has withdrawn into himself.

I stand next to the bed and do not touch him but notice his shoulders moving slightly.

I notice he's traveling and seems to want to communicate with me.

"Are you okay?" I ask.

"He only wants good for us," Mr. Samuels says. *"He can handle an unlimited amount because he has unlimited love and I feel love in his presence. It's a beautiful force. This is the best I've ever felt,"* he adds, echoing other patients. *"It's as if I've been given godliness myself. Imagine if you're standing on the beach and the sun's rays are perfectly focused on you. It makes you feel special and perfect."*

Mr. Samuels continues breathing calmly.

"I am at peace. I feel whole. Do you have faith?" he asks me.

"Yes, I do," I answer.

"It's what makes miracles and is all around us. If you pay attention, you'll feel its calm and vital energy. But if you dismiss it, you're missing out on a power that's available to all of us, that we can so easily tap into."

"How do we do that?" I ask.

"Just be still, and when it approaches, take it in. It will hold you and it exists to make us better and help ease our way."

"What about our souls?" I ask. "Do they travel to different places in the universe after we pass?"

"Your soul is available to ascend to multiple realms or move to any experience, free to go to seek its beauty and expansion. It is totally unrestricted. Our souls seek infinity within the beauty of all that is. What you refer to as different places within the universe is nothing more than the ability to access the most complete version of All."

"How should we look at death?" I ask.

"You're held in its arms and you feel safe. It's like being held by hands that are full of love and grace, held lightly but completely. I know I will be safe forever and feel complete."

"Are there stages to this process?"

"Yes, you get lighter and lighter as you ascend and it feels better and better. It's all beautiful and perfect."

"How do we understand the different levels and stages we encounter?" I ask.

"These are deep levels of experience and each is meant to allow our souls to expand, and to encounter deeper states of being, deeper experiences of love, and more profound states of knowledge. You're impelled through these encounters and totally enthralled at each stage, since each one is limitless and transformative."

This is a lot to consider. As I sit there, it occurs to me how few people would believe this man, lying unconscious in bed, is actually telling me this information. It's extraordinary evidence, whether or not everyone believes it.

The time passes and I sit quietly beside Mr. Samuels, as he continues his journey. He is at peace and at one with the process. Later, I thank him for his help and wish him peace and ease. As I prepare to leave, I also thank him for sharing his wisdom with me. Like other patients I sit with, these messages are profound, inspiring, and honor a magical aspect of the human experience. He "winks" as if to say, *"We shared something special."*

Sacred Reflections

According to some traditions, the soul may leave the body at death, but it takes time to reach higher states. These states seem to be unlimited realms of the afterlife, and we pass through several on our way to our final destination.

The patients I sit with journey to many realms. These are dimensions that reach higher and higher, are more light-filled and ethereal, and this process seems consistent with the elevation of our souls and the blossoming of our consciousness. Those who are dying know they're going on a journey and are at ease with that. As they're gradually brought along, moving higher in stages, they incorporate the love and expansion.

We have work to do to leave this life. Our bodies and spirit know how to do this, and as we travel through ever higher dimensions we are guided by the universe in the process. Perhaps another way to think of death is as a journey in which we move slowly, enjoying every step, never alone, always expanding, and surrounded by love.

Lesson Twenty-Five: We May Will Ourselves to Die

One beautiful Monday afternoon, when the sun is shining, but the humidity is low, I grab some takeout lo mein and wonton soup for lunch from a Chinese restaurant. The person at the takeout counter drops a fortune cookie in my bag, and later, I break it open and read: *Today it's up to you to create the peacefulness you long for.*

It's a message we all receive one way or another, fortune cookies aside. I hope everyone feels the peacefulness I try to create in my life, including through my work at hospice.

Since the facility's been particularly active, I've been working three shifts a week for the last month. Twenty deaths occurred in the last week alone.

This morning, as I walk up the hill to the entrance, I pass an elderly woman sitting in a wheelchair.

"Can I help you?" I ask, but she says she is fine and waiting for her ride.

Once inside, I greet the guard—a new one today. He nods silently to me and I continue on to the nursing station. When I pick up the patient roster, I see it's been reduced to a small sliver of paper, only listing the patients' names and room numbers. Their religion, diet, the day of admission, length of stay and their medical data are missing.

"New HIPAA guidelines," the nurse says in response to the blank look on my face. "No more information about the patients."

This means I will know even less about each patient I sit with. This doesn't sit well with me.

A patient wants to die

Four patients need a doula, so I head to the first room, but the patient has a woman visitor, so I move on. The second patient, in room four, has his door closed, so I don't knock. Instead, I head to the next room, room twelve.

I peek in and see the patient, Mrs. Aberman, is alone. I center myself, breathe in, and knock lightly, preparing to enter the room. As I push the door open, I introduce myself and ask permission to come in.

No response.

I take a deep breath and focus on simply being present. I enter the room, wondering what is on the other side of that door.

The scene is all too familiar. A hospital bed with electrical controls to raise or lower sections of it sits in the middle of the room. A long tray with a vertical arm and a bedside stand is next to the bed. The patient is on her back, her mouth open, an oxygen tube in her nose. There is a quiet gurgling in the room coming from an oxygen tank in the corner. Several chairs have been pulled up next to the bed.

I'm comfortable with the silence as I walk in.

There is nothing on Mrs. Aberman's end table or dresser except for four boxes of tissues. Someone must have collected these boxes for the family and visitors. The rest of the room is bare.

I pull up a chair and notice the bag of urine hanging from the patient's bed. There's not much output and what's there is dark. I know this as a sign of impending death. That said, Mrs. Aberman seems comfortable. Every once in a while, she takes a deeper breath and her breathing in between breaths is prolonged. Unlike some patients at end of life, she is quiet and seems content.

I listen to her breathing and rearrange her covers, then adjust the bed slightly. I gently hold her hand. Her energy is reedy and waning.

I'm not sure how old Mrs. Aberman is, but if I had to guess, I'd say she's in her eighties. It's hard to tell at end of life when our physical nature seems to leave and recede. Her hair is grey and pulled back in a bun. One foot sticks out of the bed and I pull the covers over it.

When I look up, I notice her husband in Spirit beside her. He lightly holds her hand, which seems to provide comfort. I ask how he is.

"I'm fine but I want my wife to be comfortable," he says. *"I've been with her a long time, these past few years. We've never been separated."*

"You're bridging both worlds," I say.

"Yes, I would do anything for my sweetheart," he says. *"This is what I need to do."*

"Did you settle into the afterlife?" I ask, curious, since he seems to have spent most of his time tending to his wife. "What's it like?"

"When you first get here you're in a space between earth and heaven, where everyone checks in. It's a big area and it's part of the afterlife but a lower vibration than where the rest of us exist. It's a lovely place and everyone feels safe and complete. No one is made to feel like they don't fit in. Everyone is administered to with loving and gentle hands."

"What happens after that?"

"After they've adjusted and become accustomed to it, they are gently taken or sent to a space that's just right for them. Here they rest and spend time, although there is no time here. The ones who need more feelings of safety and love receive that."

"Then what happens?" I ask.

"When you're comfortable and acclimated, you go to do your work. You meet others, you may get involved in higher work, like helping those on earth. You may get assignments, whatever is challenging and special to you. Whatever is most important to you is what you'll go into."

"When do you see your loved ones on the other side?" I ask. "As soon as you arrive?"

"We're with you when you pass and we take your hand and go with you to the first stage on the other side. You know we are with you. We

surround you with our loving presence so you feel protected. At least several of us are with you so you always feel completely supported. After that, when you move on, you are part of our community and our ties of love. We are all engaged with each other. We all feel the links that keep us all connected. It's like a chain of love that extends over the whole heavens and connects all of us."

I notice a noise at the door and look up. A heavyset woman stands in the doorway, dressed in white, wearing a wide-brimmed hat, as if she's in Boca Raton, not Baltimore. I introduce myself but she says, "Don't touch me. I just had an operation. But I can bump elbows." She leans forward and clicks her elbow against mine.

"This is what she wanted," she says, pointing to the patient. "She could have lasted another two years but she wanted to be with my uncle. The doctor said if she took her medication she'd be fine, but she didn't want to. This is what she wanted," she repeats. "I'm her niece," the woman explains. "She married my father's brother. He passed away four years ago. Come here," she says and signals for me to follow her out to the hall.

We walk to the end of the hallway to a small seating area with two comfortable chairs.

We sit across from each other and she pulls out her cell phone and begins to scroll through her pictures. "Here's my uncle and aunt on their wedding day," she says, as she points to a picture of a youthful man in a tux and an attractive woman in a long satin wedding gown. They're surrounded by attendants.

"And here's my father," she says proudly, pointing to another picture. She scrolls through more pictures and shakes her head as if to say, *I don't understand why my aunt wants to leave.*

We chat for a few more minutes. Then she says, "Well, since she can't talk, I'm going to leave."

"She can still hear you," I say. I want her to know that, even though her aunt looks unresponsive, she can still connect.

"Really?" she asks.

"Yes." It's important people know their loved ones likely can hear them, even when they seem unaware of their surroundings. "Watch her fingers, or her eyelids. They may move slightly as you speak. But don't expect a response," I caution.

She follows me back to the room, but looks at her watch. "My husband will be here soon." But then she looks over at her aunt and tentatively begins to speak. "Aunt Sophie, it's Ruth." She says it again, louder this time, thinking her aunt doesn't hear her.

"She can hear you," I say.

"I love you." She begins to tear up and quickly turns away.

"Thank you," she says to me and rushes out of the room.

I sit down again, glad Mrs. Aberman's niece has come. The patient seems comfortable, not at all agitated. Her breathing is steady and even, although the space between breaths is lengthening.

I sit for another thirty minutes, and then notice the volunteer across the hall has stepped out of the patient's room. She signals for me to join her, so I step out into the hallway again. Sometimes we doulas take a break and so may chat with other doulas for a few minutes. The two of us chat about being doulas, working with the families. After a few minutes, I return to the room.

As soon as I step into the room, I sense the change. I glance at Mrs. Aberman. She isn't breathing. I begin to count and get up to 100. She's still not breathing.

I make my way down the hall to the nursing station thinking this didn't come as a surprise. She so much wanted to leave and when I left the room after her visit with her niece, she passed through the door.

"The patient in room twelve has passed," I tell the nurse.

"Thank you. We'll send someone," she says.

I return to the room and wait. The woman's soul drifts out of her body and begins to leave as she makes her way slowly to the other side. This is what she wanted. Her husband drifts along next to her.

As a doula, I've had many patients who have passed as I sat with them or when I got up to go to the nursing station, or to speak to someone or move on to another room. Many doulas say they've never had a patient die in their presence. I'm not sure why that's the case for some and not for others, but perhaps the patients sense I'm so close to the other side that it seems okay with them to leave.

In a few minutes, the nurse enters the room and asks for the time in order to pronounce death.

"It's 4:20," I say.

She adjusts the patient, moves the bed down and positions Mrs. Aberman's hands over her chest. She looks at ease.

Sacred Reflections

Intention plays a role in how we live, and it also appears to play a role at end of life and death. It even appears as if individuals can will themselves to die, particularly if they feel they have nothing left to live for.

It's also known we can die of grief. There's even a syndrome, called "broken heart syndrome," which has been labeled and cited for at least 3,000 years. The syndrome includes physical damage to the heart. According to this syndrome, the individual was previously healthy, but then the heart begins to mimic the signs of a heart attack, even though there is no evidence of blocked heart arteries. This is an extraordinary example of the mind-body connection at work and illustrates the role of intention at end of life.

Anecdotes surface about long married couples who die within days or hours of each other. In this case, Mrs. Aberman wanted to be with her husband. She willed herself to leave and was more than ready to pass, suggesting the power of the mind is formidable. She left with grace and ease, on her own terms, journeying with her beloved husband to the afterlife. This is what she wanted.

Perhaps the lesson here is that to live and die with intention, honor our soul and its deepest needs, is our work here, and part of our soul's contract in life and death.

25 Lessons the Dying Teach Us About the Afterlife

Lesson One: Death is Not About Dying. It's About Living

Lesson Two: Death is a Process Involving Body and Soul

Lesson Three: Families of Hospice Patients Need Support, Too

Lesson Four: We Retain Our Senses at End of Life

Lesson Five: It's Impossible to Predict When Death Will Occur

Lesson Six: Our Chakras Transform at End of Life

Lesson Seven: The Soul Leaves the Body to Journey at End of Life

Lesson Eight: There is Something Larger That Exists and We Are All Part of It

Lesson Nine: Living Well is at the Sacred Center of Life and Death

Lesson Ten: Our Soul is Intact at End of Life, No Matter What Our Physical Condition Is

Lesson Eleven: Having Conversations About Death is Important

Lesson Twelve: It's Important to Let Go of Your Expectations of a Person at End of Life

Lesson Thirteen: Never Assume the Dying Cannot Hear You

Lesson Fourteen: Our Loved Ones in Spirit are Waiting in the Wings at End of Life

Lesson Fifteen: Family and Friends May Deal With Death Through Denial

Lesson Sixteen: You Never Know if That Last Breath is Their Last Breath

Lesson Seventeen: Each Passing is Different

Lesson Eighteen: We Feel Loved, Peaceful, and Safe as We Journey to Higher Realms

Lesson Nineteen: We May Mention an "Appointment" to Keep at End of Life

Lesson Twenty: Personal Items Add Energy and Love to a Patient's Room

Lesson Twenty-One: Granting Permission to Die Is Implicit

Lesson Twenty-Two: Angels and Celestial Caregivers Assist Us at End of Life

Lesson Twenty-Three: Synchronicity Exists in Life and Death

Lesson Twenty-Four: As We Ascend, We Pass Through Ever Higher Levels of Consciousness

Lesson Twenty-Five: We May Will Ourselves to Die

Part Four

Consciousness at End of Life, at Death and in the Afterlife

We have a fascination with death. We don't understand it, and to most to us, it signals not only the end of our physical bodies, but of us.

Certainly, there is no consensus of what is death. According to the scientific definition, it's the cessation of all vital functions including the heartbeat, brain activity, and breath. Clinical death is the medical term for the termination of blood circulation and breathing. And the legal definition means an individual has sustained either irreversible cessation of circulatory and respiratory functions or irreversible cessation of all functions of the brain.

The commonly accepted views of death are that a person is dead when all brain functions cease or after their heart stops beating.

These definitions of death leave out the religious and philosophical definitions, as well as the spiritual and metaphysical ones. So while science points to physiology as an explanation of death, this doesn't seem to address all the questions we have about what death is and what it means.

We'll probably never have a unanimous agreement on the question of death. And strangely enough, we have no unanimous agreement on the definition of life either. The two most important aspects of our experience on earth and we still can't agree on what they are.

But one explanation that I have seen and experienced in my work is that death is part of a continuum, not an end as so many believe. That it's grounded in the grander plan of the universe, and that at death, our energy continues in an essential and permanent form. This encompasses the concept that we are actually one with the Spirit realm and that the idea of separation is an illusion.

As I move between worlds and have experienced in my work, death is not the end. There are invisible worlds all around us from which infinite streams of energy flow, moving through and connecting us with the vaster universe.

Life and death are one big package—a continuum. We use our physical senses in one, and exchange them for higher sensibilities in the other. Perhaps that's why when I sit with patients at hospice, I'm not surprised when I see families in Spirit or see the near dead journeying. To me it all seems to be part of one long sequence, like the history of mankind or the evolution of the universe or an eternal timeline.

If we understood consciousness, we would go far in understanding the meaning of death. If we understood consciousness, we would have a different understanding of our lives, our place in the universe and the meaning of our existence.

Before I began this work as a death doula, I was a believer that consciousness survives physical death, but what happens in the moments leading up to death were still open-ended questions for me. As a doula, I learned that contrary to popular perception, death is not a specific moment, but a process.

I believe it's time to revise our view of death to include a broader definition. Since the scientific paradigm does not provide all the answers, or encompass the scope of what transpires, I believe it's time to include a broader definition. But I also recognize this is a tough proposition since many of us do not accept the concept of other realms of existence beyond this one.

When it comes to the question of where we go when we die, as both a doula and a medium, I've witnessed how our physical bodies no longer serve us at end of life. However, our bodies are the least important part of "us." Where we go is alive with energy and populated by everything in the most meaningful and fulfilling way, although certainly not in the physical context we seem to require to associate with life.

Life is an enduring journey. The afterlife is not a postscript. Yet, our difficulty explaining or understanding this concept rests in our difficulty explaining or comprehending life after death in the context of "life" as we know it. Our idea of "life" is irretrievably tied to our physical body. Since no consensus exists about what either life or death is, the whole proposition is up for grabs.

What I Learned As a Death Doula

I had no idea what to expect when I began my work as a doula. But the work soon turned into a transformative proposition to acknowledge the mysteries and miracles I had seen and been aware of, now revealed to me in a new way.

These hospice patients taught me there is no dying but only a journey that comes as naturally as birth. When I lose sight of what's important, this helps me.

I learned there's a sense beyond physical life—a presence. A spiritual and nonphysical existence that is in fact very real. Of course, as a psychic/medium I knew this, but as a doula, I saw the process and its meaning in another way.

I also learned that the choices we make and our beliefs are what form our journeys. Through this work, I found that laid out before me was everything it is to be human, and what living a life and death really mean.

While we are on earth, we have an opportunity to build our souls, to develop our essence. When we enter the afterlife we take that with us and move on to serve in a different way, making larger contributions. We are all here learning lessons. Every one of us. This is part of our work.

The Meaning of Living and Dying

I entered this work believing I wasn't afraid of death. That I wanted to be of service as a bridge from one path to another. Through this work, I've found that there is much to learn about the dying process—and about life too.

Each patient taught me something about living and the meaning we make of our lives. About the faces of faith and belief, and what ultimately defines us.

Not only does our essence survive death but it participates in the type of existence we will encounter on the other side. Our beliefs are reflected in the dying process right up to and through the moment of death... and afterwards.

Serving as a doula gave me a new, richer understanding of life and consciousness, a new depth to my visions and work. Of course, many will say that we can't know for sure. Or that it's what we've always been told. That death is the end.

Yet, I learned there is an existence that remains outside our comprehension, a spiritual and nonphysical existence that is real. Of course, as a psychic/medium I knew this, but as a doula, I saw the process and it's meaning in another way, up close.

Because of this work, death doesn't have the sense of finality that I used to associate with it.

As I said before, all of us are on interconnected journeys. Our higher awareness connects pieces of the puzzle, and organizes and intersects with them and other broader realities of the seen and unseen worlds. But throughout, there's something that never changes, that's eternal. This quality that defines us can't be ignored. We have a chance every day to make the best of our lives, the best of ourselves, and leave an imprint on the universe and on others.

This is one of the great powers of the universe at the end of the day.

Note to Reader

Thank you for reading *Diary of a Death Doula*. My sincerest hope is that you derived as much from reading this book as I have in creating it. If you would be so kind to take a moment to leave a review on Amazon or elsewhere, I would be very grateful. Reviews and referrals are vital to an author. To be among the first to learn about new releases, please visit my website for news, recent posts, to sign up for my newsletter or inquire about readings:

http://www.DebraDiamondPsychic.com.

Thank you again for your kind comments and precious attention.

All my best,

Debra

Book Club Discussion Guide

1. Did you enjoy *Diary of a Death Doula*? Why or why not?

2. Have you read similar books on this topic? Did the book fulfill your expectations? Why or why not?

3. How would you briefly describe the book to a friend? Is the book's central theme compelling and persuasive, or improbable and questionable?

4. What observations are made in the book? Does the author examine cultural, spiritual or religious beliefs? Does this seem appropriate or is it unconvincing?

5. What differences from your own thoughts and beliefs on end of life and dying do you find most difficult, surprising or unusual to understand?

6. What are some of the book's themes? How important are they? What issues or ideas does the author explore? Are there any other themes or concepts that should be considered?

7. How do these issues affect your life? Directly, on a daily basis, or more generally? Do they affect them now or sometime in the future?

8. What evidence does the author use to support the book's ideas? Is the evidence convincing... definitive or... speculative?

9. Did the actions of the characters seem plausible? Why? Why not?

10. If one (or more) of the characters made a choice that had moral implications, would you have made the same decision? Why? Why not?

11. Are there long- or short-term consequences to the issues raised in the book? Are they positive or negative... affirming or frightening?

12. How controversial are the issues raised in the book? Who is aligned on which sides of the issues? Where do you fall in that lineup?

13. What did you already know about this book's subject before you read this book? Do you feel the book helped enhance your knowledge and understanding of the subject?

14. Talk about specific passages that struck you as significant— or interesting, profound, amusing, illuminating, disturbing, sad...

15. What other books have you read by this author? How did they compare to this book? Would you recommend this book to other readers? Why or why not?

16. What have you learned after reading this book? Has it broadened your perspective about a difficult issue— personal or societal?

Heart of Tantric Sex
Diana Richardson
Revealing Eastern secrets of deep love and intimacy to Western
couples.
Paperback: 978-1-90381-637-0 ebook: 978-1-84694-637-0

Crystal Prescriptions
The A-Z guide to over 1,200 symptoms and their healing crystals
Judy Hall
The first in the popular series of six books, this handy little
guide is packed as tight as a pill-bottle with crystal remedies for
ailments.
Paperback: 978-1-90504-740-6 ebook: 978-1-84694-629-5

Take Me To Truth
Undoing the Ego
Nouk Sanchez, Tomas Vieira
The best-selling step-by-step book on shedding the Ego, using the teachings of *A Course In Miracles*.
Paperback: 978-1-84694-050-7 ebook: 978-1-84694-654-7

The 7 Myths about Love...Actually!
The Journey from your HEAD to the HEART of your SOUL
Mike George
Smashes all the myths about LOVE.
Paperback: 978-1-84694-288-4 ebook: 978-1-84694-682-0

The Holy Spirit's Interpretation of the New Testament
A Course in Understanding and Acceptance
Regina Dawn Akers
Following on from the strength of *A Course In Miracles*, NTI teaches us how to experience the love and oneness of God.
Paperback: 978-1-84694-085-9 ebook: 978-1-78099-083-5

The Message of A Course In Miracles
A translation of the Text in plain language
Elizabeth A. Cronkhite
A translation of *A Course in Miracles* into plain, everyday language for anyone seeking inner peace. The companion volume, *Practicing A Course In Miracles*, offers practical lessons and mentoring.
Paperback: 978-1-84694-319-5 ebook: 978-1-84694-642-4

Thinker's Guide to God
Peter Vardy
An introduction to key issues in the philosophy of religion.
Paperback: 978-1-90381-622-6

Your Simple Path
Find Happiness in every step
Ian Tucker
A guide to helping us reconnect with what is really important in our lives.
Paperback: 978-1-78279-349-6 ebook: 978-1-78279-348-9

365 Days of Wisdom
Daily Messages To Inspire You Through The Year
Dadi Janki
Daily messages which cool the mind, warm the heart and guide you along your journey.
Paperback: 978-1-84694-863-3 ebook: 978-1-84694-864-0

Body of Wisdom
Women's Spiritual Power and How it Serves
Hilary Hart
Bringing together the dreams and experiences of women across the world with today's most visionary spiritual teachers.
Paperback: 978-1-78099-696-7 ebook: 978-1-78099-695-0

Dying to Be Free
From Enforced Secrecy to Near Death to True Transformation
Hannah Robinson
After an unexpected accident and near-death experience, Hannah Robinson found herself radically transforming her life, while a remarkable new insight altered her relationship with her father, a practising Catholic priest.
Paperback: 978-1-78535-254-6 ebook: 978-1-78535-255-3

The Ecology of the Soul
A Manual of Peace, Power and Personal Growth for Real People
in the Real World
Aidan Walker
Balance your own inner Ecology of the Soul to regain your
natural state of peace, power and wellbeing.
Paperback: 978-1-78279-850-7 ebook: 978-1-78279-849-1

Not I, Not other than I
The Life and Teachings of Russel Williams
Steve Taylor, Russel Williams
The miraculous life and inspiring teachings of one of the World's
greatest living Sages.
Paperback: 978-1-78279-729-6 ebook: 978-1-78279-728-9

On the Other Side of Love
A woman's unconventional journey towards wisdom
Muriel Maufroy
When life has lost all meaning, what do you do?
Paperback: 978-1-78535-281-2 ebook: 978-1-78535-282-9

Practicing A Course In Miracles
A translation of the Workbook in plain language, with mentor's
notes
Elizabeth A. Cronkhite
The practical second and third volumes of The Plain-Language
A Course In Miracles.
Paperback: 978-1-84694-403-1 ebook: 978-1-78099-072-9

Quantum Bliss
The Quantum Mechanics of Happiness, Abundance, and Health
George S. Mentz
Quantum Bliss is the breakthrough summary of success and spirituality secrets that customers have been waiting for.
Paperback: 978-1-78535-203-4 ebook: 978-1-78535-204-1

The Upside Down Mountain
Mags MacKean
A must-read for anyone weary of chasing success and happiness – one woman's inspirational journey swapping the uphill slog for the downhill slope.
Paperback: 978-1-78535-171-6 ebook: 978-1-78535-172-3

Your Personal Tuning Fork
The Endocrine System
Deborah Bates
Discover your body's health secret, the endocrine system, and 'twang' your way to sustainable health!
Paperback: 978-1-84694-503-8 ebook: 978-1-78099-697-4

Readers of ebooks can buy or view any of these bestsellers by clicking on the live link in the title. Most titles are published in paperback and as an ebook. Paperbacks are available in traditional bookshops. Both print and ebook formats are available online.

Find more titles and sign up to our readers' newsletter at
http://www.johnhuntpublishing.com/mind-body-spirit

Follow us on Facebook at https://www.facebook.com/OBooks/
and Twitter at https://twitter.com/obooks